STEVE

THE ANSWER !

This Book proposes is !

All CHRISTIANS ARE CAlleD TO Lo...

NoT TO CommAND !

THERE ARE NOT Enough

REAL LEADERS IN God's

ARMY, BuT THERE ARE

Too MANY SELf-Proclaimed

CommANDERS.

AlwAys RemEMBER

CommANDERS HAVE SUBORDINATES

LEADERS HAVE Followers.

A Fellow Follower OF CHRIST

Are You Destined To Lead?

A Biblical Analysis of

Leadership Skills and Principles

By

Chief Warrant Officer-4

Ray Fairman, PhD

United States Marine Corps (Retired)

1963–2005

Christian Soldier (Active Duty)

1962–Present

iUniverse, Inc.
New York   Bloomington

Are You Destined to Lead?

A Biblical Analysis of Leadership Skills and Principles

iUniverse books may be ordered through booksellers or by contacting:

iUniverse
1663 Liberty Drive
Bloomington, IN 47403
www.iuniverse.com
1-800-Authors (1-800-288-4677)

ISBN: 978-1-4401-2981-0 (pbk)
ISBN: 978-1-4401-2982-7 (cloth)
ISBN: 978-1-4401-2983-4 (ebk)

Printed in the United States of America

iUniverse rev. date: 03/11/2009

First Printing April 2004

"All that is required for evil to prevail is for good men to do nothing."

– Edmund Burke

"The mantle of leadership is a cloak that rides heavy on the shoulders of those who are selected to wear it.

– *"Gunner" Ray Fairman*

"To lead with honor, a man must always perform his duty to the best of his ability with conviction, courage, and compassion; he can never do more and must never do less."

– "Gunner" Ray Fairman

Let's get started. Saddle up and read on, McDuff, read on.

Contents

Dedication

This work is dedicated to all the true leaders under whom I have apprenticed. Those who have, through their excellent depiction of biblically based leadership, instilled in me the desire to leave behind a legacy of leadership and mentoring in lieu of a monument or a comparable reputation. When my Lord and Savior sees fit to sound recall and order me home, I will respond to that call with a glad heart and a willing transfer of responsibility to that next generation of leaders who hold the following Latin phrases, which I have held so dear during my lifetime, in high esteem:

In Deo speramus, Semper Fidelis, Firmus in Christo and Sic Semper Tyranus.

Therefore, I also dedicate this effort to them, those future leaders who possess and exhibit the desire and the courage to make every conceivable effort to carry on the vision of leadership with which I was entrusted, a vision to provide strong guidance to both the leadership and discipleship efforts of our Lord's church and their fellow citizens. You see, it is those leaders who will eventually carry this dream far beyond anything I can currently even imagine. Finally, I dedicate this book, as always, to My Lord and Savior, who continues to provide for me all that I need through the Holy Spirit.

Foreword

How many of you realize that every Christian has a God-given responsibility to demonstrate active Christian leadership not only in their chosen profession, whatever God has ordained that to be, but also in the world in which they live?

Please take note that I referred to their profession. I, for one, do not feel that I have dedicated nearly forty years of my life to something I could simply refer to as either a job or an occupation. So if that's all you consider whatever you do every day to be—just a job—then maybe you should review your current career pursuit.

There are three words people typically use to tell others just what it is they do to earn their keep in this world. First there is the term "job," which is often defined simply as a task. Next, there is the term "occupation," which most people think of as their livelihood or how they earn their pay. Then there is the more stylish term "Profession," which usually indicates a chosen field of endeavor that requires a substantial amount of formal training and the subscription of its members to a written code of ethics and often to a lifetime of dedication and sacrifice. Professionals are generally considered to operate at higher performance levels simply because their vocational requirements are being motivated by their avocational desires. I consider myself to have been pursuing a "profession of arms" in one uniform or another ever since I walked out of high school in Southern California in June of 1963.

I feel that, just like the ministry, the legal, medical, technical, and many other service-oriented professions are in fact very demanding on their members and require a definite calling. There are many good men and women who are just not cut out for the hardships and strain that being a dedicated professional can and will put on their lives and families.

Nor are they ready to accept the fact that this means willingly serving every single person they encounter along the way. You must understand that, when you are a true professional, you are not in business merely to make a living, but to provide the very best service of that particular kind that you can to all those who are in need of your efforts. I would like to reinforce that premise, right here. In order to do so, I must and will direct you to the Law Enforcement Code of Ethics, a professional document that I was required to memorize and recite along with my oath of office as a law enforcement officer when I first entered that profession in the late 1960s. I was required to swear to uphold the spirit of that code as well as its written codified principles when I first began that phase of my adult life, also in Southern California. That Code of Ethics has never changed over the many decades I have spent in law enforcement and still begins with the phrase "As a law enforcement officer, my fundamental duty is to serve mankind..."

I would also like to point out to you that God has directed each and every one of us who responds to a call to lead others, to do so with the goal of service as our focal point. (Law enforcement officers may want to look at Romans 13:4.)

It is essential that all leaders understand a key point regarding having the right attitude before they ever undertake their leadership journey, so please take a moment to consider this next statement carefully. Christ Himself, though God, thought it not beneath Him to empty Himself of His divine power and take on the person of mortal man in order to accomplish all that provides for our salvation. Can you imagine the distance He spanned in leaving His deity behind and taking on the form of a mortal man in order to secure our salvation? (See: Philippians 2:6–8.) If that is not showing a desire to lead from the front, then I guess I never learned a single thing about leading others during my career in law enforcement or as a Marine Corps Officer.

Now, are you really ready to respond to God's calling for you to lead others in your life? I mean lead with a true, heartfelt desire to provide not only direction and service, but also to exercise a kind of leadership that is balanced with compassion and discipleship toward those you serve and those with whom you serve?

Before you answer, let me ask you another question. How many of you feel you are already fully qualified to accomplish those leadership tasks right now? Be careful and first think about how you will answer because, even after forty years in one type of uniform or another, thirty-nine years behind a badge, forty-two years of military service, and more than forty-five years as a Christian, I still don't always feel absolutely, positively, and completely qualified. However, somewhere on my journey along the leadership trail, I came to understand that God didn't want me to wait till I felt totally qualified to accept his commission to lead others, and neither can you! If we were fully qualified to do anything on our own, we would not need God and then He would not be able to use us, for it is through our weaknesses that His strength shows through. God has called all Christians to lead, especially to help lead others to Christ. That alone requires—and should inspire—you to learn just what it takes to truly be a Christian leader and step to the front.

I know some of you can't seem to believe that God really wants to use you; but take my word for it; God loves to use all kinds of people to perform His work. He frequently depends on reluctant, unqualified and *FAT* (*that's Faithful—Available—Teachable*) people like you or me to accomplish His work, and He always has. You will learn that if you wait until you feel fully qualified, you will more than likely feel you are capable of handling God's mission without His help, an act that not only steals His glory but sooner or later results in disastrous consequences.

Have you ever taken a close look at biblical leaders like Moses, Jonah, Jeremiah, or David? Those of you who have realize there are countless biblical leaders who had feet of clay and obviously felt unqualified to lead when they were called to leadership. Yet God chose, trained, and directed many of these folks to accomplish some of His most important missions.

If you already feel like you are the perfect leader or "Jewel Encrusted Golden Chalice," as I like to call that type of person, then you are likely to be viewed with awe, maybe even revered. You will possibly be placed on a proverbial pedestal and seldom used. You might even become so heavenly-focused that you will turn out, as the saying goes, to be of no earthly good. It is also quite probable that you will be a chalice that will never leak. You will never have to be refilled with the Holy Spirit. When you are filled with blessings to the rim and then there is no room for any more, you'll wonder why God has stopped giving you blessings. It will most likely be because you have never passed any of those Godly blessings you have received along to anyone else. Who is going to benefit from all your accumulation? Anyone? No! That's why I really believe God loves to use the common man or "Cracked and Earthen Chalice" to serve His purposes. I believe the common Christian makes the best leader because he has already learned how to follow—follow Christ, that is—with a broken boldness, boldness that keeps pride and self-sufficiency from distorting truth and reality. I tell you truly, it is a wise man who remembers that the praise and flattery the world offers is, like perfume, something that should be sniffed and not swallowed.

Sometimes when I take time to look at the world around me, I feel like I am living in a twenty-first century Book of Kings, where, though good leadership and bad leadership both abound, the ugly fact remains that bad leadership seems to be prevailing. I believe that today, in both the church and in our society, we are desperately in need of the solid Christian ethics of a few good, strong and dedicated leaders.

I also contend that our country still has a fairly solid grip on morality, which is, philosophically speaking, the knowledge of right and wrong. We are, however, erring badly today by taking so many detrimental shortcuts and detours as we trudge down the road, guided by "situational ethics." We are all too quickly and easily swayed by the opinions of those who favor doing what is politically correct or personally profit-able. What ever happened to being morally courageous? Or just plain correct?

Today, more than ever, it requires courage to step forward, defend what is morally and ethically correct, and let the chips fall where they may. You might say that's a job for a real warrior. Well, my God is a God of war, says the Bible. The Bible is a document where Christians are often likened to soldiers, especially in Ephesians. So, if we are truly called to be soldiers, and even leaders, should we then quietly and compliantly whimper off into the shadows whenever the going gets tough, and the world attempts to redefine our acceptable moral and ethical standards for us? Who will we ultimately answer to, the world or our Lord, God, and Savior, Jesus Christ?

I want take a moment right here to quote Thomas Jefferson because I love the way he once put the answer to that rhetorical question regard-ing the concept of moral courage. He stated *explicitly,* "In matters of fashion, swim with the current. In matters of conscience, stand like a rock."

I feel it is time we stop wavering and acquiescing to the pressures of this age of tolerance and eventual acceptance, where the protecting of feelings and reputations is frequently more highly valued than the proclaiming of truth. Though I believe firmly in facing these conflicts, I do, however, advocate proclaiming the truth with compassion, for it is never my place to judge; that privilege and responsibility is reserved for God and jurisprudence. Nevertheless, you and I are sure to be con-fronted with situations that will call for us to form and maybe even affirm opinions and we will be held responsible by God for acting on those opinions in the same way Jesus would act. I don't know about you, but I don't need a bracelet or a T-shirt to remind me that Jesus would always DTRT (Do The Right Thing)—my pocket reply to the WWJD craze.

Since your leadership capability generally determines not only your own level of effectiveness, but may many times impact the effectiveness of others, isn't it time for you to raise the bar on that leadership? If you think it is, then you need to begin to develop and exercise the kind of transformational leadership that is biblically based. So isn't it time to adopt a powerful leadership style that is based on character, conviction, and Christ-likeness?

Yes, the need is great and the hour is late, but there is still time for transformational leaders to influence today's world. A legacy of good leadership is the best inheritance you can leave to future generations.

I have studied God's word over many years, and I have discovered that a multitude of leadership qualities, traits, profiles, and principles lies within the covers of the Bible. These truths are patiently waiting to be discovered and integrated into our everyday lives. Dealing with any of these areas in its entirety would require me to develop the equivalent of at least a semester course at a Bible college. So I only intend to take you on a micro-journey exploring some of these biblical leadership traits and principles that I have attempted to integrate into my own Christian walk.

Now, with all this in mind, let's take a look at some of the leadership lessons God has placed in the Bible. Lessons we can learn from some of His devout professional leaders.

What we are going to look at during this leadership journey is twenty-one lessons complete with examples and the scriptural documentation to substantiate them. I want you to realize, though, that reading about these principles and traits and not taking the time to study them in depth or meditate on them or act on any of them will not do you any heavenly or earthly good. If you really want to become the leader you were destined to become, you will need to work on strengthening any character weakness you might discover along this expedition and implement any of these principles you might have overlooked in the past. Always keep in mind that, ever since the fall of Adam and Eve, it has always required an effort on the part of someone to accomplish either a good or an evil act.

No matter what your occupation, position, or current assignment is, you need to recognize that your missionary and service opportunities are endless. Never forget the old adage: "You may be the only Bible someone ever reads." What proof will the defense have to work with in heaven, when your life's testimony is offered up as evidence of your faith in, and service to, our risen Savior?

Let's get started. "Leaders to the front!" Remember, you can't learn to swim on the beach!

Chapter I

Pre-mission Briefing

People have often accused me of speaking or writing over the heads of my audience. Those critics feel I should lower my expectations for those who listen to me or choose to read what I write. They just don't seem to understand Marines. We just don't look at things that way. I feel that if I can influence people to exercise, they will grow stronger, and if that philosophy holds true for their physical bodies, it must also apply to their character and intellect as well. So, as you prepare to read this book, get ready also to get actively involved with the manuscript. Argue with me, agree with me, or disagree with me. Write in the margins, use a highlighter, challenge my ideas, or feel challenged by them, but don't read the book and stagnate. Growth is dynamic and contagious. I have been growing as a leader for many years, and my growth has not happened by chance, luck, or accident. I have learned and am still learning more every day about what leadership is all about and how to improve mine by trial, error, effort, observation, education, and the grace of God.

I'll bet some of you are already sitting there wondering, just who the heck is this guy and who gave him the right to call himself a leader? Well, the process started in May of 1963 when I joined the United States Marine Corps just before graduating from San Marcos High School in Santa Barbara, California. My recruiter, Gunnery Sergeant Leroy Steiner, would not let me leave for boot camp until I finished the last semester of my senior year. He told me that a career in the Marines would require a good bit of discipline, determination, experience, and education, as well as courage, especially if I desired to become a well-trained Marine Corps leader. He was oh, so right, but he failed to tell me it would take a lifetime for me to realize that leadership is not a destination but a continuous expedition.

My leadership journey was slow but steady until it took a real leap during my last Vietnam tour. When I made Staff Sergeant in 1969, I was in Chu-Lai RVN, Southeast Asia. At my promotion celebration, my Sergeant Major told me that I was following in the footsteps of a long line of strong Marine Corps leaders who had gone before me, and I told him that I had learned something from my Marine Corps Master Sergeant father about Staff Non-Commissioned Officers that I felt was even more important. He asked what that might be, and I told him that leaders didn't generally follow in anyone's footprints; they blaze their own trails where not many men have gone before.

True to the ways of my beloved Corps, the next day I found myself a brand-new SNCO, leaving the safety and security of my F4B Phantom squadron, VMFA 314, based at Chu Lai, and taking over as the acting platoon leader of a Defense Platoon operating on the Batangan Peninsula in Quang Ni Province. There, for several months, I blazed trails where not many men wanted to blaze trails.

I was a young hotshot who thought I knew a lot about leadership, but as I soon found out, I still had so much more to learn.

By the time I made S/Sgt, I had already endured many hours of leadership training and even held some noncombat leadership positions. I was a good follower, a pretty good mission accomplisher, and I had already served in combat. But as a rising leader, I found that I had not completely internalized a few principles that are, beyond any shadow of doubt, vital to my God, my family, my country, and my Corps.

It is vitally important to understand that, having a degree, title, rank, or position alone never qualifies a person to lead anyone anywhere. Even knowledge, experience, and age do not automatically make a person a quality leader. If you truly desire to lead, you must become the kind of leader that people want to follow. When you reach that decision in your life, you also need to be willing to accept the responsibility of trading privileges for sacrifices. Yes, I have heard that "RHIP" garbage about Rank Having Its Privileges, but what rings even louder in my ears is "RHIR"—Rank Has Its Responsibilities. I still had to learn that my leadership would not only determine my own effectiveness, but, more often than not, directly impact the effectiveness of my unit and other Marines. This fact served me well during the decades I spent following my active and reserve military career and would serve me just as well in my subsequent career in law enforcement, as I was eventually to learn.

I would like to take the opportunity in this book to share with you just what I believe it takes to become a real leader. These will be only some of the things I learned during my Marine Corps career—a career that spanned forty-two years and two combat theaters. It makes no difference to me if you plan to pursue a career in the military or if you plan on having a career in the civilian world; these principles will benefit you anywhere you apply them.

You need to begin by understanding that real leadership is a privilege and not a right of the position you hold. Leadership must never be taken lightly. It will always be earned and awarded; it should never be regarded as just being given, because when that occurs it becomes "deadly" obvious to all concerned.

Chapter II

The Confidence of Gideon

The leader who desires to acquit himself well must naturally exude confidence, a trait that must never be confused with arrogance. When beginning the climb toward a position that entails the administration of certain powers, the embryonic leader often starts from a position of reluctance. Eventually, with the proper seasoning and experience, the leader arrives at his or her destination with the level of confidence required of that position. All too often, however, there remains the danger of allowing that confidence to take on a life of its own, especially when it is allowed to feast unfettered on the fruits of its labors. When that feasting occurs, it often has a way of morphing the personality of the leader into that of the dreaded "arrogant moron."

A Journey from Reluctance to Confidence

Let's begin our journey by looking at the Old Testament passage of **Judges 6:1–8:35**, where we will discover a great example of a somewhat reluctant leader, yet one who turned out to be quite an effective force in the long run. I am talking, of course, about Gideon. He was an obscure man from one of the weakest of the minor Israelite clans—a man who never envisioned himself as a national leader. Yet he was clearly called and used by God to overcome the Midianites in the most asymmetrical victory in Israel's long history of battles. How could this have occurred? Well, I have a few ideas regarding Gideon and his leadership, which I would like to share with you.

First of all, Gideon wisely began to develop and display his leadership in his own home. In spite of intense opposition that even threatened the life of his son, with ten of his servants he destroyed an altar to the false god Baal and constructed an altar to the One True God. If we desire to perfect our character and enhance our leadership capabilities, we, too, must begin this process in our own homes. Let me take the time right now to ask you a direct question—only one of many I may ask as we progress along our leadership journey: do you accept the God-given responsibility for the spiritual state of your own life, home, and family? If a man cannot find the courage and discipline to face the challenges of providing godly leadership in his own home, where love abounds, with his own family, how will he ever be able to lead in an environment of strife and conflict, where the resistance to his guidance is often so plentiful?

Gideon also took the time to garner the support and confidence of a person of critical influence. He did this with charisma and appropriate behavior, before he began to display or exercise any authority as a leader. Moreover, he was wise enough initially to broaden his "sphere of influence" among the people of his own region. It is a well-known fact that as a person's popularity grows, so does his or her influence and credibility. If you doubt that this is true, you merely need to take a critical look at the impact that politicians, sports figures, Hollywood actors, rock stars, and the rest of the world of celebrities and entertainers has on our society and the development (or devastation) of its moral and ethical value definitions.

Gideon's maturing leadership and confidence eventually influenced so many people that, in retrospect, it is easy to see why, in order for God's power to be the dominant factor in this victory; God had to have him send a great number of his followers home. Yet it is also clearly visible why, acting under God's direction and timing, and with insight, is also very important. For it was by having Gideon follow some simple steps to mature his leadership and gain support before taking over that God used Gideon's ability to win a great battle and victory with only 300 combat troops.

I like to refer to Gideon's leadership contribution as "The Lesson of Self-Assurance," though others may merely want to call it "self-confidence." You see, Gideon knew that people must somehow visualize you as a leader before they will ever agree to follow you. He was also ready to answer a critical question all followers are sure to ask: "Why should I follow you?" That is a question that you, too, must always be prepared to answer.

You see, until people are confident about the value you place on your character and can see how important character truly is to you, they will never feel confident about anything you envision, no matter how worthy a goal it seems to be. This is because people are looking for some very specific character traits in those people in whom they choose to invest their confidence and trust.

Let's take a closer look at some of those traits, shall we? People are usually looking to follow someone who not only wants to "lead from the front," but can also demonstrate a "calling and ability to lead." Sometimes emotion alone can send someone into battle, but that emotion can never sustain their effort. What is required is that a person who desires to lead exhibit a bold, passionate, and confident attitude without developing an arrogant, pompous, egotistical, or self-important attitude. This is not always easily accomplished, and it is an attitude that generally takes a concerted effort to maintain.

Subordinates are also looking for leaders who can display a "heightened degree of insight"—a characteristic that is frequently exemplified through a person's wisdom and vision for what lies ahead.

Another important factor is a person's "charisma," which is most often detected in a leader's ability to make people feel valuable and good about themselves and their accomplishments.

People also want to follow only those leaders who can show them that they are both "technically and professionally talented." After all, you can't learn to tap-dance from a plumber, and you don't expect a ballerina to repair the transmission on your Volkswagen, do you?

One of the most important traits looked for by followers is also one of the most difficult to acquire. That skill is the ability to remain a part of the team while leading it. You are going to hear me say this more than once and in various ways, but I feel it is that important. You can ride to victory on the shoulders of those you lead or be trampled beneath their feet. The choice is yours, and the difference is determined by the leadership styles, methods, and principles you choose to employ.

You will never be able to lead successfully unless you have developed good communication skills. You must count the ability to listen among the most important of the skills you use to communicate. You need not always act on what you hear, but if you ignore the feedback you are receiving, disaster is often only a heartbeat away. I will also tell you right here, and likely again somewhere later along the line, that killing the messenger will never change the message, nor will it ever change the pending consequences. It only sends you into battle one more man short and leading a unit of reluctant followers with lower morale.

Last, but certainly not least, people want to follow leaders whom they feel they can continue to look up to—leaders who display a stable moral and ethical character. A properly adjusted moral compass will always point the way toward the foundations of trust that are required by all successful leaders, even those who are reluctant and seem to lack confidence, like Gideon, at the outset of their careers.

Just be sure that you keep a tight rein on your maturing confidence, or it is apt to turn into a malignant arrogance and destructive self-sufficiency.

Now take some time to read and thoroughly study the referenced passage on Gideon.

Chapter III

Assessing Samuel's Power of Credibility

In **I Samuel 4:1** we learn a little about a leader named Samuel. Whenever this leader spoke, the people always heard the truth. Samuel was one of the most credible leaders chronicled in the Old Testament. His rise to prominence began under his mentor, Eli. Thoroughly studying this leader will reveal that eventually this leader outshined his mentor, but he still incorporated a little of his predecessor's baggage along the way. I say this not to demean Samuel—God forbid; I wish I was half the leader he was—but merely to show that none of us will ever reach perfection until we see Christ in person. No matter what the message was that God wanted him to proclaim or reveal, Samuel could be trusted to speak only the truth. Yet whenever Samuel spoke this truth, he always spoke it with real compassion and conviction. I know from past experience that truth delivered without compassion can frequently be counterproductive and devastating.

You might, therefore, call Samuel's contribution to our leadership lexicon "The Lesson of Compassionate Credibility."

Any leader who reaches a point in their life where their input is sought after must realize that they have also arrived at a pinnacle of immense responsibility. This ought to require them to review their values, motivations, and actions in light of at least four critical leadership responsibilities. Let's take a quick look at these four areas of accountability.

First, we need to consider an area we will call "Shepherding." The key to examining this area is the accurate and honest evaluation of a person's leader-subordinate relationships. A leader must clearly understand that the relationship of a shepherd to his flock is an allegory for the relationship of a leader to his or her subordinates. Can you see you or your current leader acting or developing in the way the Lord teaches and desires us to lead? Do you know, love, protect, teach, and guide your subordinates? A good leader does. I once worked for a sheriff who took the time to greet every man and woman in his agency by their first names. Not bad in a small department, right? Sorry, folks! When he retired there were over 800 men and women in that office. Never take lightly the imagery of a shepherd; remember that the Lord is our "Shepherd" according to the Bible. See **Psalm 23** for your responsibilities.

Second, let's take a look at the area of "Stewardship." Our primary focus here should be on developing dependability. You see, exhibiting your fidelity toward those whom you desire to lead is a crucial way of illustrating the steadfastness of your position regarding the management-subordinate relationship. While it is true that you are always accountable to your leaders, you are also always responsible to God for the actions you take on your own behalf or on behalf of your subordinates. Therefore, you must always be faithful to Christ while maintaining your integrity in all your dealings, with both directions of your Chain-of-Command. This is because God, superiors, and subordinates will ultimately hold you accountable for the way you manage what has been entrusted to you and that includes the lives and spiritual well-being of all those you encounter.

Next we need to look at the "Vision" required of a leader. The focus of our evaluation this time is on revelation. Leaders must have a clear vision and be able to communicate that vision to those whom they lead—and even, at times, to those whom they follow. They will frequently need to bring that righteous vision to bear on contemporary issues, just as Samuel did. There will be times when you must be the bearer of bad news. At those times you must seek to find ways to communicate that unfortunate information honestly but with the greatest compassion. You must also lead with conviction during those difficult times, using the wisdom gained from past experiences, present situations, and even your insight regarding future possibilities. When you lead in this visionary manner, people *will* follow.

Last, but not least, we must take a look at the mandates for "Servanthood." This will not be the easiest of the evaluation requirements, will it? Well, the major focal point here will be rights. You may not like to hear this, but biblically informed and well-seasoned leaders will generally be found abdicating more and more of their own rights, the higher the leadership position to which God elevates them. That is because, as a committed leader, you will more often than not find yourself sacrificing your own rights or privileges for the good of those who follow you. If you are primarily motivated by power and not service, people may follow you for a season, but they will not follow you for long. I have heard it said many times in many different ways, and so have you by now, that you can be carried to victory on the shoulders of those who follow you or be trampled beneath their feet when they eventually catch up to you. The choice is yours, so make it, and make it well known. Once you have decided whom you consider the most important, will you tell them or show them? I know I'd rather see a sermon than hear one any day.

God has called everyone to join His army and a selected number of us for promotion to positions of leadership within that army. Every leader in God's Army needs to be a servant, and remember; we were called to lead, not to command. Servant-leadership is difficult for some of us to understand because it requires such a high level of selflessness. That is why God has not, nor will He ever, elevate every servant to the heights of leadership. Yet, even as a simple Christian soldier, you are a leader who will someday find yourself being the reason or the excuse for the way people respond to, or behave in relation to, the example you set.

Do you still want to climb that precarious pyramid of leadership? I hope so, because the world is in dire need of real leaders. If you still want to be a leader, you need to remember that to be a successful leader in God's kingdom you must adhere to biblical principles and work within the ordered system under the authority of God. While a king (or a presidential candidate) can be a maverick, you as a leader cannot. You must be a trustworthy communicator, an example, a servant— under the conviction and authority of the Holy Spirit. That's all there is to being as credible as Samuel. Are you ready to comply?

Chapter IV

Sampson Had an Obvious Need for Integrity

In **Judges 13:24–16:31**, we meet Sampson, a leader who provides us with a stellar example of bad leadership. While it is not my customary procedure to use negative examples to drive home a point, God tells us that *all scripture* is profitable, so I am going to rely on that principle of truth while I attempt to point out some of the potential pitfalls that may be experienced when a leader decides to forgo a foundation of integrity and live by deception, as Sampson was prone to do.

All leaders are endowed at birth with the innate potential to become either a good leader or bad leader, and Sampson was no different. He had numerous opportunities to make the proper choices, just as every leader does. Each of the decisions a leader makes results in success or failure and adds to or detracts from his or her personal reputation.

Take a moment to reflect on just exactly how the summation of your current reputation might be expressed by those who really know you. I can tell you what that reputation is made up of; it is the sum of your confidence, competence, and character, and can be wrapped up in one very valuable leadership trait that Sampson seemed not to understand—integrity.

We will therefore call Sampson's contribution to our leadership lessons—a contribution that is most evident by its absence from his poor style of leadership—the Lesson of Integrity.

Integrity can easily be referred to as the keystone of high-quality leadership. You see, people are usually prone to forgive and maybe even forget (though the two are definitely not synonymous) occasional lapses in ability, as long as they can see and believe that a leader is readily accepting responsibility for his or her actions and mistakes and continuing to grow. However, what they can't and won't forgive or forget are continual or even occasional lapses in a leader's character. Even the slightest slip of character damages the bonds of trust between leader and follower. This is especially true for the fledgling bonds of trust that are being forged by a new or maturing leader.

Sampson could have been one of Israel's greatest leaders if he had not succumbed to such additional character flaws as impetuosity, volatility, moodiness, lustfulness, unpredictability, and emotionality. In the end, nobody follows a leader he or she cannot trust. In fact, people will cling to the memories of these lapses in order to justify their own shortcomings at later times. This concept eventually came to be called the "You can't fault me or hold me accountable for following your example" defense.

Can you identify the signs of a leader in trouble? Let's see how well you do on a quick analysis of some of Sampson's key indicators. Poor leaders will more often than not fail to address their own glaring character flaws, thus allowing their detrimental effects to spread like untended physical infections. I think you will all recall how the Scriptures admonish a person to remove the plank from his own eye before undertaking the surgical procedure of removing a splinter from the eye of another. *When moral and ethical character flaws are left untreated, they will depreciate the infected character until it virtually no longer exists.* What actually does remain is simply put: bad character. Who among you has the desire to follow a leader with bad character? Sampson's frequent use of prostitutes and selection of a pagan wife, his definitive relationship with Delilah, which was based on deception, and his violent tendencies all contributed to his leadership debacle. As you should clearly see from Sampson's example, the disease of weak leadership is an infection generally born at home.

Leaders, who are counting on a game plan of deceit to protect them, and to prosper, will eventually be consumed by their own machinations. Although in our society it often appears that disobedience and deceit are currently held in very high regard by troubled leaders in both the church and society. These malignancies seem to be joined at the hip with these leaders' vocabularies and activities. The degradation of the truth through the use of "omission" is just as injurious to a leader as committing the outright act of prevarication. The end result will always be distrust and betrayal. These are not really the sort of underpinnings on which you can build a relationship. Never forget that the Gospel is the Truth and the Truth will make us free. (See: **John 14:6**: "Jesus saith unto him, I am the way, the truth, and the life: no man cometh unto the Father, but by me.") (KJV)

Impulsive leaders will often rush headlong into trouble, just as Sampson's rash wagering, matrimonial choices, and aggressive attitude ultimately led him to his downfall. It seems apparent to me that leaders who cannot control themselves or their emotions endanger not only their own dreams and future, but those of their followers as well. Their mission—and ultimately they, themselves—will likely end up as casualties when leadership is sacrificed to the rational gods of self-centered privilege.

A myopic preoccupation with a single character flaw will eventually result in the total disintegration of character. No matter how gifted untrustworthy leaders are, they will eventually meet their match. This is true because a corrupt, immoral, and unethical lifestyle will in due course consume anyone who partakes of even the most nominal of its delights.

Sampson was a leader who seemed to thrive on deceit, yet he was himself defeated by Delilah, the ultimate embodiment of deception. It is always wise to remember that focusing on minutiae restricts the vision of any leader and may eventually cost them everything, as it did Sampson.

Not using—or misusing—God-given gifts, especially they are used for purposes other than those God intended, will eventually lead to the downfall of any leader, no matter how well established or popular they seem to have become. Sampson took for granted his anointing as a judge and his God-given strength, gifts which were provided for the deliverance of his people. We are all aware of how that turned out. Unwise or self-centered leaders will surely encounter the same type of disastrous consequences when they ignore or divert their God-given talents toward the striving for positional power, popularity, personal gain, or political expediency.

Leaders who pride themselves on leaning on their own understanding are routinely undisciplined, arrogant, and self-centered leaders who have frequently lost touch with reality. A leader who becomes a legend in his or her own mind is most often only a leader in the same jurisdiction. Such leaders have also lost their desire to be taught, and, since leaders are required to be teachers, and the best teachers are lifelong learners, unteachable leaders become a liability not only to themselves but also to any organization of which they may be a part.

Poor leaders will consistently fail to learn from their mistakes, while good leaders view mistakes as the milestones of a person's achievement. Leaders, like everyone else, must learn something from every decision they make. To do this, they must be courageous enough to take calculated risks but wise enough to avoid unnecessary risks. They must remain humble enough to admit errors, honest enough not to blame others, sensible enough to correct their errors, and secure enough to listen to sage advice.

Poor leaders are also more prone to the use of reaction instead of action. When leaders wait for action to become necessary, it means they are merely responding to a stimulus. Leaders, by virtue of their title alone, are required not simply to respond but to initiate actions in accordance with their mission vision.

Poor leadership is often easily defeated. This occurs because poor leaders are too afraid or too stubborn to change their character. They will suffer defeat after defeat, thus bringing upon themselves depression and resignation. They never seem to realize the meaning of the scriptures when they teach us that, "Greater is He that is in me than he that is in the world."

The world will likely never know how much it could or would have benefited, if our historical Sampson-like leaders had used their God-given talents wisely instead of selfishly.

Chapter V

Barnabas, Teaching the Art of Delegation

In **Acts 9:27** we are introduced to a man named Barnabas. This man was a leader who was secure enough in his own capabilities and in his relationship with the Lord that he was willing to empower others to act in his name.

It is a well-documented fact that insecure leaders, or micromanagers, as we tend to call them today, generally closely guard their own power at all costs, eventually leading to their own personal devastation. More secure leaders, on the other hand, will often accomplish more and greater things by consciously and willingly empowering others under their command or influence to act on their behalf. They do this by proportionally delegating their authority to their followers, a course of action that depends to a great degree on their subordinates' acceptance of responsibility. By utilizing this principle, they can lighten their own burden while allowing their subordinates to gain valuable training, insight, and experience.

I suppose you could call this contribution "The Lesson of Delegation," which not only empowers subordinates but also conveys to them that their leader's confidence in them and concern for the success of their joint mission transcends his or her own need for recognition and glory. This is viewed as a positive signal that shows subordinates that leaders are concerned more about a legacy of leadership being passed along through those they influence than they are with any accolades they themselves might ultimately receive.

A leader can never be so afraid of being replaced that he or she fails to train those under their command to become qualified to do exactly that—replace them. You see in many thriving organizations you advance only by training your replacement, while you are being trained to succeed your current leader. United States President Teddy Roosevelt once pointed out that a successful leader is one who selects and empowers the right folks to do the job and then displays the necessary self-restraint to let them do the job without meddling. In short, the only indispensable person in an organization is the one who works the hardest to help others attain the level of training and experience that will enable them to replace him or herself at any time. That type of leader works to ensure the future of the organization and the fulfillment of its mission, not to ensure his or her own reputation in history.

Our man Barnabas was just such a leader. He never seemed to let an opportunity go by to uplift others. Especially obvious were his interactions in this vein with Paul. So, what do you say we take a look at several key actions he undertook on Paul's behalf?

Barnabas believed in Paul earlier than anyone else in the recorded history of the early church, which was not an easy thing to do, considering Paul's past and reputation. It is very easy to be the first to form an opinion about someone or something, but it is quite something else to be the first to go out on a limb and express that opinion. Still, if you really want to be a leader in God's way, you need to be willing to take chances on people, as Barnabas was willing to do. He didn't wait for the apostles to accept and endorse Paul. He saw the work of the Lord in Paul and encouraged him in his growth, even while others in the church still feared him. This display of faith can be a risky thing, since people may fail or disappoint you. Those who do succeed, however, as well as those they eventually influence, will never forget the person who gave them their first leadership opportunity. Think about it for a moment. Can't you still remember the first person who took that risk and gave you the encouragement and opportunity to lead? Because of my "hodgepodge" background, I have learned from several spiritual and secular leadership mentors I will never forget. These people were willing and able to see characteristics and potential in me that others—and sometimes even I—did not then see. They took the risk necessary and empowered me to make the mistakes necessary to solidify my emerging leadership, never abandoning me throughout my maturing process.

As the Bible states in the referenced scripture, Barnabas "Took Paul and brought him to the apostles." He did not ask for an appointment or wait to be called, or for Paul to completely prove himself. He endorsed and pleaded Paul's case before them and described his actions, undertaken in the Name of Jesus, at Damascus. Barnabas enthusiastically placed his own reputation for integrity and leadership at stake to step out boldly and turn his opinion of Paul into an affirming action. How often do you ever place the welfare of another person above your own? Have you ever experienced this feeling? You really need to try it.

Barnabas, just like another biblical leader named Tychicus, was a leader willing to take a backseat in biblical history in order to sponsor a man whom history now records as one of the most prominent leaders in the Christian faith. I seem to recall having heard somewhere before that those who would be first must first be willing to be last. By accepting a secondary position, Barnabas was empowering Paul to fulfill God's commission to preach, teach, and record the word of Christ.

Taking this chance didn't mean smooth sailing for Paul or Barnabas would always be in the offing. We do know, however, that, with Barnabas' endorsement and the subsequent endorsement of the apostles, Paul was free to move about Jerusalem and teach and debate the meaning of scripture. Still, as one might expect, he made some enemies among the region's nonbelievers. Rather than revoke their endorsement, the apostles sent Paul back to Tarsus for his own safety and supported his preaching the gospel there among the gentiles. When you are willing to go out on a limb for someone, you will truly find out that some days are diamonds and some days honestly are millstones. A real leader who truly understands his responsibilities will not back down, though. Just remember, my friend, forewarned is forearmed. If everything was supposed to be peaches and cream after becoming a Christian—or especially a Christian leader—God would never have had the Book of James ordained, written, and canonized.

When Barnabas was assigned to help the Church at Antioch, he made it a point to look up Paul and make him his companion in that work. This assignment was Paul's first real leadership project. Eventually he made Paul his partner in missionary work, the role God had destined Paul to pursue. This tasking, as we know, eventually led to the student's surpassing his teacher. This philosophy seems to be strangely lacking support in today's competitive society, where most people seem to want to hang on to that No. 1 ranking, no matter what the consequences for the future might be.

I need to ask you a significant question right here. Are you ready, right this moment, to invest yourself in the people you supervise and serve? If so, remember that when you answer yes, it is going to require a great deal of personal sacrifice, energy, and time. I am sure, though, that if you are willing to give it a try, you will find it is well worth the price.

I retired as a sergeant from a Florida law enforcement agency after almost seventeen years of service, and at times I was even used as an acting lieutenant. I was replaced in my last assignment by a lieutenant whom I had trained when he came on the agency several years after I did. During my tenure with that agency, I served as The Field Training Officer or a supervisor for about 30 percent of that agency's eventual Command Staff. You see, I trained people to go where, for one reason or another, I never went in that agency, and it has never bothered me one bit. During my nearly forty years in law enforcement service, I have been more disappointed by my tenure with other agencies, where I was given plenty of recognition and rank but was excessively micro-managed and severely restricted in the ways in which I was allowed to train and develop the potential of those who worked with and for me. Watching others grow because of your assistance is quite honestly, a very rewarding experience, indeed. You see, I feel that a man is measured not by what he accomplishes but by what he accomplishes for and through others.

I want to ask you to take this lesson from Barnabas to heart. Why? Because he was not the only great leader to use it, as we will see when we look at another great leader who espoused this principle of delegation. It is recorded in the New Testament that delegation comes directly from Our Lord Jesus Christ. Try reading **Luke Chapter 10:1–24**. The Lord sent seventy laborers out and told them they were as sheep among wolves, but, most important, he delegated an authority in **Luke 10:19** commensurate with the responsibility He placed upon them. Will He do any less for you? I think not. Therefore, can you do any less for those whom you lead? Again, I think not!

Chapter VI

Moses Understood the Leader's Choice: Privilege or Sacrifice?

Through **Exodus 3:1–4, 13**, Moses teaches us that a leader has to give up in order to grow up and go up. I know there seem to be a lot of *ups* in that sentence, but that is because that is the direction most people who desire to climb the ladder of success eventually come to realize they have to go. They also become conscious of the fact that the climb is both predictably difficult and fraught with pitfalls. Even in the beginning, it is to them a foreign and justifiably false concept that the power and perceived freedom they will achieve as a leader can come without forfeiting anything. Leaders journeying toward the top frequently encounter obstacles to that faux philosophy. Sometimes, they will come to realize, they may have to take pay cuts, give up certain rights, or even decline superior assignments in favor of doing what is best for the organization and their subordinates. Talk to any successful leader and I guarantee you that he or she will tell you that they have made many sacrifices along the way. Leaders will sacrifice much for the betterment of all or, as Mr. Spock puts it, "The needs of the many [truly] outweigh the needs of the few." Since leadership is an ongoing process, so then, will be the need to sacrifice. Circumstances may change, but principles don't, so let's get back to Moses.

This time we are appropriately calling this lesson of his "The Lesson of Sacrifice." All honest leaders will agree on one thing, that leadership involves sacrifice. If you really want to be a good leader, you must ask yourself two critical questions, especially if you claim to be a Christian. Those questions are: what price are you willing to pay to become an effective leader, and to whom are you willing to make that payment? Will it be to God or the world (Satan)? Let's take a good look at Moses' life, since he is a fair example of one who sacrificed much and often for the work of God.

Moses gave up the power and prestige of the world he lived in, and he truly had a lot to give up in the eyes of the world at that time. As the adopted son of Pharaoh, Moses sacrificed the exact things that many people today tend to esteem at the highest levels and that some folks actuality even come to worship. Yes, you could say that Moses sacrificed the whole world for the leadership position God had destined for him. Let's see if we can find out why.

After giving up the hurriedness of the world, Moses got time to be alone with God. If he had he stayed in Egypt, do you think he would have ever heard God's "still small voice" echoing through the opulence of Pharaoh's courts? Maybe, but I'll wager God might have had to yell a great deal louder. During his forty years of exile in Midian, Moses' heart had the time it needed to quiet itself and to allow him to reflect on God's continuing call to leadership. When he finally encountered the burning bush, he found that he was at last ready to listen to the voice of God. Is your heart quiet enough to hear God's call to leadership in your life? Just what is He asking you to do? Are you willing to do it?

Like Moses, you need to be honest with God in all your dealings. God knows each of us better than we know ourselves, which may be a sobering thought if you take the time to consider all its implications. Moses knew he had his weaknesses, but he was willing to expose them to God because he had at last sacrificed the pride, arrogance, and cockiness associated with his previous powerful position. You may not find that all sacrifices you must make are this costly. This, though, was a very humbling sacrifice for one of Egypt's proudest "young guns," yet it was a vital one, for only as an older, wiser, and humbler man was Moses able to be of such great use to God.

Ask yourself a couple of questions. Are you humble enough to lead anyone? Can you stop screaming I'm No. 1 for just long enough to take a lesson from Avis? To what lesson am I referring? I'll tell you: "Try a little harder [for others] and let God worry about what you really need." He's pretty darn good at it.

As his life progressed, Moses developed an escalating hunger to serve God. Have you? If you truly have a desire to serve God in your profession, whatever that may be, then there will eventually be a battle between that hunger to serve and your own self-reliance. While it is true that you must have confidence to lead, replacing it with arrogance or self-reliance leaves God out of the equation. It took forty years for Moses to be able to focus on God and sacrifice his self-sufficiency; how long will it take you? For a Christian, this is a given. Self-sufficiency is, and always will be, an obstacle to humility and Christian leadership.

Just as Marine recruits are broken down and rebuilt at MCRD Parris Island and MCRD San Diego, Moses was broken down and rebuilt by God (who is an excellent spiritual DI). That isn't such a bad thing, as you will see. Besides, who knows you better than your Creator? When Moses was finally "kaput" and no longer hindered by pride or self-reliance, he was able to build a very strong relationship with God and in so doing became a God-reliant, rather than a self-reliant, individual. Are you relying on God in all things that you do, or are there still times when you hope God is really too busy to hear or see what you are doing or saying? By the way, you do realize that it is often your fears that God wants to break through, don't you? Fears you have about yourself and your capabilities to lead. Remember, it is God who empowers and uses the weak to confound the proud. It is usually those whom God would use who are truly the most fearful. Moses doubted his own value. Have you ever questioned your own purpose or value? God wants to calm those fears and set you free to use the gifts He gave you. He will assure you of the purpose of your life if you will only allow Him the opportunity.

If you have some fears concerning God, try reading **Galatians 5:22–24** and tell me that those qualities are something to fear. Yes, my God is a God of war, but he is also a God of compassion. Never fear that He can't keep those two personalities in perspective.

You may be harboring some fears concerning just how others will respond to your attempts to become a leader. Well, if I remember correctly, Moses got caught up in the worry of how people might react to him. I also seem to recall hearing somewhere that if God is for you, who can stand against you? Does that sound familiar to you, too? Give God a chance to demonstrate what his power and commitment can do through you, and remember, it is not you doing the work, or at least it shouldn't be; it should be God working through you. Remember this: "To God be the glory; great things He has done"?) (Hymn: To God be the Glory—Fanny J. Crosby [1820-1915])

If it is fears concerning your ability that are troubling you, then look at these fears directly through the eyes of Moses, who had tremendous fears about being able to do God's work. I am sure that you will see that your fears, like those of Moses, are based on an assortment of earthly reasons and may reoccur at diverse times throughout your remaining life.

But every time Moses posed one of these fears to God—and I am sure he did that on a regular basis—I'm sure God merely smiled and raised up an appropriate leader to complement Moses' insecurities. Leaders like Aaron and Jethro and Joshua. What evidence can you provide that indicates God can't supplement your abilities however and whenever He sees that it is necessary?

With your willfulness broken, fears overcome, and purpose reaffirmed, you are ready to place your life and leadership in the hands of God. Hold lightly to the things He gives you, as there may be a requirement to someday trade them off in order to move up to a higher calling. If you truly desire to lead, you must be willing at any time to answer the call to sacrifice. Never forget, though, that you can never out sacrifice Christ.

Chapter VII

Elijah and Elisha Knew the Impact of Personality

In **II Kings 2:1–15**, we learn from Elijah and Elisha, who were both good leaders, that the exercising of good leadership will attract both the loyalty of other good leaders and a higher quality of followers. Today, a person with this capability is referred to as "charismatic." Sometimes people like these are dangerous because they have nothing of value to sell, but they sure can sell that nothing with gusto.

My experience over the decades has taught me that the kind of people you attract is much more likely to be dependent on what type of a person you are than on what you have already accomplished or want to accomplish in the future. I find that people tend to draw closer to people who they feel are a lot like them. If you are an, "I am the most important part of this team," type of leader, then imagine what it will be like leading a band of folks who feel the same way about themselves. If, however, you are the kind of leader who is willing to sacrifice for the benefit of others, think of how much you will be able to accomplish with followers who are willing to give their all to ensure the success of your vision.

I have chosen to refer to this as "The Lesson of Charisma," and this gift is present to a varying extent in all leaders, both good and bad. Every person is born with an instinctive need for affection, recognition, and a sense of belonging. Observing a person's innate hunger to find something or someone to follow or emulate most easily demonstrates this need. As a result, even the weakest leader, one who has even the smallest desire to lead, finds him or herself with some quantity of followers. Why does this occur? That natural desire we humans are instilled with to gather, will always result in some folks following and some folks leading, whether qualified or not. This is something that every leader needs to remember, because every leader, whether good or bad, is also following someone or something.

A leader's style also induces people to follow intellectually, emotionally, or volitionally. The greatest leaders, though, will amass their followers on all three levels, via their minds, their hearts, and their wills. This is just what Elijah did when he defeated the prophets of Baal. Not only did he call down the fire from heaven to consume his sacrifice, a feat that intellectually convinced even his most confirmed skeptics, but he also drenched his sacrifice with copious amounts of water to increase the difficulty of what he was petitioning his God (and mine) to do, or so thought his audience. It seems obvious to me that, with God's help, Elijah knew just how to play to a crowd, just as a good leader sometimes must play to his subordinate audience. Elijah also showed that he connected with the crowd's will when he commanded them to seize the prophets of Baal and then watched as the crowd complied.

Effective leadership in and of itself is neither good nor bad, as it must always be channeled through the leader's moral and ethical filters before it can be recognized and labeled. Try evaluating the leadership of the following list of ancient and modern leaders: King Saul, King David, Adolph Hitler, Genghis Kahn, Mother Teresa, Billy Graham, the Lord Jesus Christ, your supervisor, and you.

It is really fairly easy for nearly any leader to attract admirers or followers who are similar to themselves; however, it takes a strong leader—and one who understands and accepts and deals with his or her own weaknesses—to readily attract and properly utilize people with different yet complementary abilities. Never forget that a leader who fears competence in others is usually insecure and harbors some fears regarding his or her own growth.

Just like all the other traits we have and are about to discuss, charisma can be styled, cultivated, and matured. This is primarily accomplished through interaction with others, as regards the leader's vision and purpose.

Charisma—or magnetism, as I have heard some folks refer to it—is more than just having the right personal chemistry. There are at least four key elements that must combine in order for it to function effectively. The essential factor in all four elements is defined by the word "mutual." These elements are vision, expectations, contributions, and commitment. Look at the examples below of "mutuality."

> a. Elijah and Elisha shared a vision to serve God.
>
> b. Elijah had expectations for Elisha, who in return had expectations of Elijah.
>
> c. While they were together, they shared in their contributions to each other and to God.
>
> d. Their commitment to each other can be seen in Elijah's three-time offer to release Elisha and in Elisha's three-time refusal to be released.

You can tell a lot about the quality and value of your leadership when you check out the following you have attracted. Whom have you fascinated and why? Would you want your kids to marry any of them? Do you recall that old saying, "It's hard to soar like an eagle when you are surrounded by turkeys"? The good news is that if you see that you want out of the flock you have currently gathered, and you are willing to expend the required energy, there is still time to change, mature, and revamp your leadership style and to paraphrase **Isaiah 40:31**, "Mount up on wings as eagles, run and not be weary, walk and not faint." Also remember that if you are comfortable with the turkeys gathering around you, you better start thinking about being someone's Thanksgiving Dinner.

Chapter VIII

Rehoboam and the Battle of
I and Me vs. We and Us

Amalgamation. I'll bet you just never spent much time thinking about that word and what it really means, have you? Well, when we finish this session, I think it might just be a more important tool in your leadership toolbox.

Once again, I am forced to use a negative example as a training example, but I guess at times they do serve a purpose. Once, when I was feeling somewhat inept and depressed, one of my subordinates (a lieutenant) told me that all was not lost. He said I "could always serve as a very good bad example." I guess I never ruled that advice completely improvident. Thus, I come to this important chapter with a second negative example.

If we read **I Kings12:1-24** carefully, we can learn a few lessons about how not to lead, from Rehoboam—a good example of a somewhat "egocentric" leader. You see, Rehoboam was a leader who had a very hard time ever getting beyond connecting with anyone but himself. He did very little to attract and endear his followers to him. I feel that we can learn great lessons by examining and analyzing our own failures, so I guess that's why I have chosen to refer to Rehoboam's leadership contribution as "The Lesson of Amalgamation."

As you study the referenced scripture, you will find out that Rehoboam was a leader who was much more interested in flexing his own political muscle or clout than actually developing any leader-subordinate relationship with his people. It seemed to me as I read that section of scripture that applying the unifying principles of teamwork was unquestionably a foreign concept to Rehoboam. (We Marines have a saying that has today spread across many venues, especially the sports world. It goes, "There is no I in TEAM.")

I stand firmly convinced that, to become a good leader, you will frequently be required to make some sacrifices that, for some strange reason, seem to be very alien to a lot of so-called modern-day leaders of our society. These foundational sacrifices, however, are absolutely necessary in order to truly connect with those you lead and those you serve. You need to remember always that those two terms (*lead* and *serve*) are not mutually exclusive; in fact, they are much more closely related than most people care to realize.

Okay, now let's look at some of the things that, in my humble opinion, you *must* do to really develop a united leadership team and avoid the negative impact of maintaining only individual connections, shall we?

The first thing you need to learn to do is to "get beyond yourself." This is easily illustrated by observing your ability to leave the "RHIP" (Rank Has Its Privileges) philosophy in the background, while drawing the "RHIR" (Rank Has Its Responsibilities) philosophy to the foreground.

I believe it was Albert Schweitzer who acknowledged that a people blessed with the knowledge, health, talent, and ability to lead should never let selfishness or insecurity develop a gulf between themselves and those whom they are privileged to lead. Getting beyond yourself also means being able to see and evaluate yourself a bit more realistically than others may tend to judge you. You must not only remember, but also believe, that to sacrifice for the needs of others is not a duty or an obligation, but a responsibility and an honor. Never forget that positions of leadership are—and should only be awarded—based on performance and capability, and should be viewed as a privilege and never as a right.

Another leadership standard you must adopt is the willingness to absorb and grow through the wisdom of others. They say that a wise man learns from his mistakes. If that is true, then how much wiser is the man who learns through not only his own misfortunes, but those of others. If Rehoboam had taken the time and sought to learn from the experiences of his elders, he might have discovered that he still had quite a number of things to learn about leading. But this cocky, young, unteachable leader failed to recognize a chance to learn and consequently to grow, thereby eventually leading his nation into disaster. It is my contention that, as knowledge and experience are gained, they are stored statically (like water in a reservoir), just waiting to become the proud parents of wisdom. Wisdom requires that knowledge and experience be put into action in order to produce wise results.

In order to ensure that you will always have something astute to pass along to others, look for something to learn from everyone and every circumstance you encounter. As the rules of crime-scene evidence state, every encounter with another is an opportunity to bring something in and take something else away. So never allow these opportunities to connect with people and to learn escape your consideration.

Good leaders will always give beyond themselves. When you focus, like Rehoboam, only on what you can get for yourself, your potential becomes stagnant or stationary like a lily pond, not dynamic and vibrant like a raging river. That means you are going nowhere and doing nothing, which is often a sign of low self-esteem, which can frequently be accompanied by a shorter life expectancy.

Leaders who know where they are going will always go beyond themselves. You see, though connecting with others is not complicated, it will always take some effort and sacrifice on your part. This requirement for personal sacrifice is what so often becomes a leader's undoing. Focusing on the singular "I" instead of the plural "we" is a prerequisite in planning for defeat. Ask yourself this question: "Who will ultimately ensure my success—I alone or those I properly train, motivate, and watch out for?" It is hard to motivate others unless you remain open to their needs. Wise leaders are always attuned to the needs of those who follow them but must also be wise enough to realize the difference between the real needs and the perceived needs and desires of those followers.

If you as a leader consider the importance of giving first and then accepting the giving of others, you will see the benefits almost immediately. One example I use to illustrate this concept is near and dear to the hearts of all police officers. (I can use this example without fear of being accused of stereotyping, because I served more than thirty-five years as a law enforcement officer.) The example I will use is one that even children can understand. Imagine that I have a box of doughnuts with just enough doughnuts for everyone in the room to have one except one person. I ask what the result will be if I take a doughnut first and then pass the box around. The answer is usually the same. The group tells me that one person in the group will be left out. Then I ask what the difference will be if I do not take a doughnut myself but elect to pass the box to the others first. They point out to me that I will have no doughnut. Then I ask who in the group would offer me a small piece of their doughnut, since I gave out all the doughnuts and left myself out. I usually end up with enough affirmative responses to result in my receiving two to three times more doughnut than anyone in the group. Leaders must believe that to cast their bread upon the waters will indeed result in it being returned sevenfold.

Truly caring for individuals gains the attention and respect of crowds. However, playing to that crowd and only paying lip service to caring for others will eventually be exposed for just what it is—manipulation and exploitation. Those are not the character traits required to build a leader a firm foundation based on trust, are they?

Leaders who are not reactive and are truly interested in building a winning team will reach out to their subordinates, who will then reactively reach back to them, thus completing a cohesive and permanent bond of brotherhood that can only be described as teamwork.

Whether you are in a new leadership position or have been in one for some time is of no consequence. You must believe that it is never too late to start leading others toward more successful accomplishments by following some of these biblical principles. Remember that the measure of a good leader can be found not in what he or she has accomplished single-handedly, but by what they have accomplished through others.

I want to end this chapter with an old toast I heard while serving in the Middle East in the Marine Corps. It goes something like this: "When you came into the world, you cried and the world rejoiced. Live your life and lead others in such a manner, so that when you are finally called home, the world will cry and you will rejoice." This will only happen if you learn to stay connected with those you lead.

Chapter IX

Deborah Appreciated the Gift of Deference

In **Judges 4:1-16** we can learn a lesson from the distaff side of life as we gain knowledge about the leadership of Deborah, a strong and respected Israelite leader.

Most of us are, or should be, aware of the fact that unspoken and informal leadership more often than not exists in every organization. Whenever and wherever people congregate, you can almost always stand off to the side and observe the posturing or testing of the waters, so to speak, by that unofficial leadership. The strongest of these leaders, even when not officially empowered, will tend to make a few tentative moves, assess the results, and prioritize their impact, then position themselves as they feel comfortable. By the time they finish, you can easily recognize those people who will set the tone for, and control, the gathering. Merely by observing these reactions, even the most casual observer can identify that natural leadership. This is a natural occurrence because it is normal even for leaders to follow leaders they respect and consider to be stronger leaders than they are.

I am, therefore, going to refer to Deborah's contribution as "The Gift of Deference." We should all know that deference (also defined as respect) can never be demanded, and neither is it conferred solely with authority or position alone; to be effective, it must be both earned and freely given.

Deborah possessed a way of actively demonstrating her leadership that subsequently earned her the respect of both men and women, something not easily accomplished by a woman in the culture of her time.

Yet even military commanders sought her help. Let's take a look at how she gained this respect from her followers.

First, you need to realize that deference begins not only with yourself, but also with those with whom you associate. In Deborah's case, people came from all over the land to have her settle their disputes. She was a judge who was well respected and whose opinions were respected, primarily because she respected herself and her own actions, and respected those with whom she worked and those whom she served. She always demonstrated this in the ways in which she dealt with everyone she encountered.

Next, you as a leader need to consistently set the bar for your own expectations higher, not lower. Always seek to exceed the expectations of others. Nobody at that time would have expected a woman to transform the way Israel lived. Nevertheless, Deborah raised the standard of living for the common man and returned the nation of Israel to peace.

Leaders who desire the respect of others must always be willing to go the extra mile, achieve their victories one at a time, and do it not for their own vainglory and elevated reputation, but for the benefit of those they serve and lead.

You will also always need to stand firm vis-à-vis your convictions and their resulting decisions. Deborah exemplified the strength of her commitment when she agreed to accompany Barak to the battle even in the face of his doubts regarding the outcome. Wise people will almost always respect a leader with strong convictions who considers him or herself to be a member of the team and is willing to join them in the journey. It is always prudent to remember that those who stand firm for nothing will likely fall for anything. One excuse I hate to hear from a leader is: "I think you are right, but I really don't want to upset the boss, so ... I just do what I am told." That sounds a lot like a Nuremberg or Abu Ghraib defense to me.

Being respected requires a person to possess and exhibit high standards of maturity and security. Respected leaders like Deborah don't need to grab all the credit and glory for themselves. They are both mature enough and secure enough to give as much as they possibly can to those who actually do the work. Remember that you can ride to victory on the shoulders of those whom you serve or be trampled beneath the feet of those you only command; the choice is yours.

Being respected does not mean that it is never acceptable to enjoy your personal success. Deborah had already seen success as a prophetess and a judge before experiencing her success with Barak and his battle. As you and your career advance up the ladder of success, accept the rewards you earn, but accept them with humility and recognition of the greater service you can perform in your new position. But never forget how your fingers once occupied the rung on the ladder of success beneath your feet.

Whenever possible, a good leader will contribute to the success of others. Deborah gave the people all they needed to succeed: a good and competent commander, the resources they required, and the infallible word of God that they would prevail. They listened, believed, and relied on both her promise and her actions and won a victory over Jabin, the King of Canaan. Just how well do you contribute to the success of your followers? Are you proud of their accomplishments or envious of them when they get recognition because of what they have done? I hope for your sake you are not your own first priority, like so many others who parrot the phrase, "If I don't look out for No. 1, who will?" If you are your own first priority, then it might be time to remember the concept of "Let him that would be first, be last." I also recall hearing something from the Bible that indicates it is always better to be called to the head of the table by the host than to be embarrassed when asked by the host to move farther from the seat of honor. I no longer need to toot my own horn; it, like Deborah's, will be tooted for me in heaven if, and only if, I deserve it.

Thinking of others in advance is indicative of a leader's talent for strategic planning. This does not mean just a battlefield ability to quickly improvise, adapt, and overcome, though that is an asset. No, this talent is even more indicative of "the 6 *P*s of Command" (prior, proper, planning, prevents, poor, performance). With the overall welfare of the people in mind, Deborah gave Barak the command to fight, a strategic plan of battle, and even accompanied him to the battle. She exhibited concern, wisdom, faith, and vision. How easy she made it for the people to respect her leadership!

How you exercise your authority over people will also have a profound impact on your gaining the deference you desire and need to effectively lead others.

There are five levels on which leaders, in general, exercise their authority, so let's look now at these levels which, of course, I will put into a military format often referred to as "the 5 *P*s of Respect."

The first *P* represents **Position**. A good leader is or should be aware that titles and positions provide the lowest and weakest level of leadership. If position is the sole basis for a person's authority, it will often result in subordinates who are following reluctantly and then only because they are being forced to comply. How many times have you yourself chafed at being told, "You will do it because I'm the boss, and I said so." Maybe it was even put more bluntly, something like, "It's my way or the highway." No matter how it comes across, authority exercised solely because of position s is seldom successful for an extended length of time.

The second *P* is for **Permission**. When followers grant their permission to a leader to be led, it indicates that there is a bond of trust being forged that will add support to the leader's position and title. This is the more effective method we should be using in the military and law enforcement arenas. In this country, we police by permission, though I will agree that at times it may not seem that way. However, if the citizens we serve were not willing to relinquish any portion of their personal or civil rights for the protection of others, then we would be professionally impotent. Our authority is based on the permissions provided by the majority of society. The abdication of some of these absolute rights will come only when the followers you lead and serve realize that you as their leader have their welfare as your primary consideration.

The third *P* is for **Production**. This next level of influence is reached when, under your leadership, the people begin to accomplish preset objectives and share in the successes together. People are now following for what you can do *for* them, not what you can do *to* them.

The fourth *P* is for **People Development**. To reach this level of influence and experience—one of the greatest of life-changing impacts you will ever know—you must help others reach the highest levels of their own potential. This may sometimes seem threatening to you if you are a weak leader, especially if the follower has a higher potential than you their leader can ever hope to achieve. Still, when you reach this level, your focus should and must change from leading and inspiring to developing and encouraging the leaders of the future. This is the beginning of the leaving of a legacy and the transitioning of your vision into a new or expanded vision.

The fifth and last *P* is for **Personal**. You can never reach this level on your own. Deborah is remembered as the mother of Israel not because she desired or sought that title but because of who she was and what she did for the people of Israel and because of how she did it. Leaders who spend their time wisely by inspiring people, training leaders, developing organizations, and concentrating their efforts on the welfare of those they lead will receive the respect, and admiration for which many others will strive a lifetime for and never attain. Leadership by virtue of who you are is the highest level of authority available and the least often awarded.

As a forty-two-year United States Marine, I recognize the contributions of all the other branches of the military, but I still take a certain amount of pride in the statement of President Ronald Reagan, who said in 1985, "Some people spend an entire lifetime wondering if they made a difference. The **Marines** don't have that problem." Will you put on that mantle of leadership today and make a difference for the future? Will you be a part of that future or a footnote in its history?

Chapter X

Jesus, the Leader's Legacy of Truth

In **Matthew 28:16-20**, we learn about leadership directly from Jesus Himself. It should be obvious to many people—and that even includes His enemies—that, at a minimum, Jesus is the leader who has had the greatest impact and left the most preeminent legacy in the history of the world. If you want to find out some of the reasons that His legacy has remained so widely recognized, then stay with me as we examine the life expectancy of the heritage of a truthful leader. For, as Jesus said in **John 8:32**, "And ye shall know the truth, and the truth shall make you free" and the Romans remind us with their ageless Latin rendition: "Veritas vos liberabit."

Jesus led with His eye on the future of His followers, and not only with His influence on the present in mind. An apparent contrast can be found in the words of American artist Andy Warhol, who, way back in 1979, made an observation that from that point in time forward people would seek to experience during their lifetime fifteen minutes of fame. That statement seems to be a comment that focuses on the importance of focusing on the present rather than the future.

Well, you budding leader, you need to consider that your fifteen minutes in the public eye, no matter how satisfying it seems to be, is so insignificant when compared to the eternity of the future that it won't even have the impact of a firecracker in an artillery barrage. I don't care how much of your life you spent in the spotlight. This is especially true if you considered the purpose of that light to be to highlight you and your accomplishments. If that is or has been the focus of your whole lifetime here on Earth thus far, then, my friend, everything you accomplished pales as twilight when compared to eternity and what Jesus accomplished.

Just how long will your memory and reputation remain? How long will you live in the hearts and minds of those who knew or encountered you along life's highway? I feel sure it will depend much more on your character and those you served (and led, not drove) than on what you did to gain the pinnacle of earthly success.

This gift our Lord left us can be referred to as "The Gift of a Leader's Legacy of Truth." To create a leadership legacy, the leader needs to think honestly, strategically, and intentionally. This can be accomplished more readily by focusing on several simple guidelines.

As a leader, always decide ahead of time just what you are willing to sacrifice to reach your goal, because being a real leader always demands that a price be paid. The mantle of leadership is a heavy cloak around the shoulders of those who choose to wear it. If you hope to have a lasting impact on the future, though, you will take every opportunity to learn from Jesus and those you lead that your life is no longer your own.

It is very important to understand a precept I learned early in my military career. This principle of leadership came to me from a wise Marine Corps Major in Vietnam named Mike Murphy, who told this new USMC Staff Sergeant that I would be wise always to remember as I progressed up the chain of command that I had a responsibility to give up so that I could teach others to go up that same ladder of success. So ask yourself, are you willing to give up your time, your money, some of your dreams and aspirations, or even some great opportunities to ensure that at least a part of your vision for a better world survives long enough to be inherited by—and to better—the lives of other generations?

If you want to help fabricate that bequest of moral and ethical leadership, then you must take the initiative. Start the process; you can't wait for someone else to start and then join in on his or her vision. Jesus often had to fight the agendas of others, and you will likely be required to do the same. Some of you may recall that the Jewish people were expecting a leader who was a warrior Messiah not a servant leader like they received. Simon the Zealot wanted Christ to lead a revolt against Rome, James and John were also a bit enamored of positions of power (see **Mark 10:37**), and even Peter tried to dissuade Christ from accomplishing the very act that was to be the foundation of the inheritance He left us today.

You also need to select the leaders you choose to mentor with goals for training them foremost in your mind. This is required because any legacy you leave will primarily be dependent on others. That means that in order for a legacy to live long enough to have an impact on future generations, it will always require the proper selection and training— or, as we say in the church—the discipleship or mentorship of the right people. This mentoring is the process of maturation imparted by the personal tutoring of those future leaders devoted to continuing the vision of their own leaders. There must be a specific development process designed and personalized for each person you select to disciple as a future leader, based on their distinctive gifts and God's goals. That is the way God worked in the Old Testament, and that is the way Christ worked in the New Testament, and I feel that it is the only way any honorable leader can work today.

Only a fool fails to prepare their followers and themselves for eventual succession. While we all will live forever (only our future address is ever in doubt), none of us will live in this mortal world forever. Once a sound leader has prepared their people to lead, they should begin the process of transition, as it may take some time for these new leaders to acclimate. We all learn best from the errors we make as we develop, and since it is easier to counsel and advise your charges while you are still around than to come back like Jesus did after death in order to fine-tune His disciples, who still had not fully comprehended their responsibilities. A leader with wisdom will always see the need to empower others while they are still developing in his or her shadow. Discipling subordinates—a term that really only indicates less mature leaders or Christians—requires that one slowly let these emerging leaders walk into the sunlight as they, the seasoned leaders, retire to the shade. A leader who will not delegate to subordinates after training them is not only unsure of those they chose and trained, but also of his or her own ability to teach and lead.

Jesus had an excellent **IDEA** (I love acronyms), which He bequeathed to us for leaving a proper legacy, so lets take a look at that **IDEA** as we transition out of this principle:

Instruction. The Bible documents that Jesus constantly taught his disciples and followers, frequently using parables and allegories to make His words more easily understood. Truthful insights were always revealed when these lessons were examined in detail. A good leader will use reality and practical application to instruct those he leads and serves. And great leaders never let an opportunity to teach others escape their grasp.

The more you sweat in training the less you bleed in combat.

Demonstrate. Don't rely solely on lecturing or the written word to convey your message; live your message. There is a poem I read once that says, "I'd rather see a sermon than hear one any day, I'd rather one go with me than merely show the way." Can you see how important it is to understand and say what Jesus said, "Come and see, Come follow me and then come and be with me"?

If everyone learned without the need for performance testing, we would need only authors and not leaders.

Experience. Christ always maneuvered his trained followers into roles of independent responsibility as He continued to add to their training, in order to combine their training with real world experience. This action indicates to me that *everyone* needs time to practice and mature their leadership styles and skill levels. A leader who never steps forward, never takes a risk, never makes a mistake, never leads, and never goes anywhere, never leaves a legacy. Sounds to me like he or she stays in never-never land.

Knowledge without experience is a static power and merely fuels a dormant leader.

Assess. Just as Jesus consistently evaluated his disciples' progress, a competent leader needs to monitor (not stifle) the progress of those under his or her care. Great leaders will consistently evaluate performance both honestly, impartially, and reasonably, celebrating their subordinates' successes and applying constructive and compassionate analysis, humanizing their followers' failures so that those future leaders may continue to learn, increase their effectiveness, and improve their overall worth.

If you train an eagle to be a turkey, it will more likely end up as someone's Thanksgiving dinner.

In order to leave a legacy, you must have someone to leave it to, who will carry it on for you. This takes the right people, the right process, and the right amount of you poured into their lives. For only when you have poured out a sufficient quantity of yourself for them will they be able to pour out themselves for others. You see, nobody can ever give of that which he has not received. The Romans would have put it this way: "Nemo dat quod non habet."

We Marines simply say: "You cannot give what you do not have."

Chapter XI

Jethro Utilized the Gift of Insight

If you take the time to really study **Exodus 18:1–24**, you can learn a valuable lesson about a critical leadership component from Jethro, whom the Bible identifies as a very intuitive leader.

Possessing superior intuition is definitely a valuable asset to a leader, but where does a person acquire this highly tuned instinct? Well, in my humble opinion, it comes primarily from two sources. The first source is as a gift directly from God. This is exemplified through one's inherent, natural ability. The second—which is a requirement for fine-tuning the intuition received directly as a heavenly endowment—is from experience, training, mentoring, and acquiring skills through extensive practical application.

Fine-tuning this trait of insight or intuition is really a process that begins at birth and continues throughout a person's life. An accomplished and intuitive leader will continue to read, to study and to learn—not merely from books, but from all the people with whom they interact, as well.

Everyone is born with certain natural instincts or talents, but not all people have natural leadership instincts. For example, a person may be gifted by God as a giver. He or she can sense when another person is in need. A person who is gifted as a prophet—or encourager, as some would prefer to label this gift—can sense when a person is in need of support, mercy, or comfort. Those who are gifted with the character traits that will allow them to become extraordinary leaders have the tendency to view and evaluate every encounter with difficulty or choice as an opportunity to grow.

Most people will acknowledge that Moses was a good leader, but I think history indicates that he was not a natural one. Nevertheless, as Moses' leadership steadily improved, so did his intuition. On the other hand, his father-in-law, Jethro, it seems, was a natural leader. When confronted with a problem unlike any he had ever before seen (e.g., leading more than a million disgruntled and displaced Israelite slaves), he seemed to know exactly how to handle the situation.

Let's look at five key things that intuitive leaders must be able to perceive on the fly.

Situations. A valuable leader must be capable of quickly sizing up any situation just like Jethro who, after watching Moses lead the Israelites for only one day, and without hiring a consultant, forming a committee, or authorizing an extensive and expensive government research project, instantly perceived the presence of an existing leadership deficiency. For a leader, the key is not always coming up with the solution to the problem, but possessing the ability to realize rapidly that a situation requires his or her immediate attention and intervention. Then he or she can initiate corrective action.

Trends. A close examination of **Exodus 18:18** reveals that Jethro rapidly anticipates where Moses is headed by attempting to do everything by himself. You might say today that Jethro reads the handwriting on the wall. He knows that if the trend continues the way it appears to be going, a disastrous breakdown of leadership will occur, resulting in defeat for the Nation of Israel, instead of victory.

Resources. A wise leader always needs to understand how to use the resources they are given to their maximum efficiency. Jethro saw just what the greatest assets were and used them as foundational building blocks in developing his advice to Moses. He saw the great desire in Moses' heart to do God's will, he saw God's favor on the Israelites, and he saw that God provided leaders among the people themselves. Thus, his plan and proffered advice were based on utilizing everything of value that was readily available.

People. The skillful reading of the motives and abilities of the people you lead and serve is always a critical factor in dealing with people. Some people who try to lead have a hard time understanding this, while others can both understand the principle and apply it. One particularly important cornerstone in the foundation of leadership is the ability of the leader to understand the difference between empowering others with your ability to read, understand, and direct your vision and simply manipulating them to accomplish your goals. You see, empowered leaders remember how they felt at being empowered, and will ultimately empower others, while manipulated people retain nothing but bitterness and resentment over being manipulated. Manipulated people learn to manipulate rather than to lead. The perceptive Jethro merely suggested that those who had the ability to do the job should be allowed to do the job. When your leadership tenure is over, do you want to leave behind a legend, a liability, or a legacy? What you bequeath to future generations will be dependent on, and reflective of, your character. Will your leadership withstand that test of time? Remember that when you leave this world, all that goes with you is your character.

Themselves. Leaders who do not understand their own strengths, weaknesses, motivations, and calling will never be able to lead anyone, even themselves. Sometimes realizing you are not the right person for the job is not only a huge blessing, and the right decision, but the mark of a perceptive and strong leader as well.

In reality, insight helps the good leader become a great leader. The Bible is filled with examples of God's ordained leaders acting with intuitive leadership. Jethro used his intuition to improve the leadership of Moses. Nehemiah merely looked at the wall in Jerusalem and knew what needed to be done and what to do. Joseph understood Pharaoh's dream and knew what it meant for Egypt and the other lands and knew how to prepare for the future famine. Whether it is naturally or intentionally acquired, intuition is a valuable tool to any leader, anywhere, who uses it wisely.

Chapter XII

Joshua Developing the Gift of Influence

From **Numbers 14:6–9** we can learn a little about a man named Joshua. Joshua was a leader who really understood the importance of being able to influence—not manipulate—others. Joshua was also a man who understood that it took time to become an influential leader, a fact all too often overlooked (sometimes intentionally) by many people who are seeking positions of leadership in our current "fast-food society."

Time, I believe, is a key factor in developing "The Gift of Influence**.**" I have met too many leaders in both my military and law enforcement careers who felt command, control, authority, or power would be the only real evidence of leadership their subordinates and superiors alike could recognize. While power and leadership are definitively not mutually exclusive, there is an old military proverb that clarifies the difference quite emphatically. It simply states what should be the obvious, and it goes like this: "Leadership is power, but power is not leadership." I learned a lot more in my climb toward humility and leadership. It has been a long and tough climb with few rest areas, so let's keep going; I'm burning daylight.

I believe this comparison of the terms *"Leadership"* and *"Power"* means that, while one true measure of leadership is the influence or authority that is vested in the position you occupy in the chain-of-command, it is also a compelling fact that leadership and influence can and should never be based on position alone. For example, in **Numbers 14**, the optimistic Joshua returns with Caleb and the other ten spies from their recon mission in the land of Canaan, the land which God had promised to deliver into the hands of the Israelites. His position as a young tribal leader is at that time insufficient, even when combined with the slightly advanced leadership of Caleb, to convince the other Israelite leaders to follow their recommendations.

Though Joshua is definitely considered a leader and holds the power commensurate with his position, at that time in his life he still lacks sufficient influence to persuade others to follow his lead.

Let's take a look at some of the factors that I feel affect the nature of a person's influence, shall we?

First let me say that I do not feel influence is unilaterally effective. I mean that just because you hold a position of leadership does not mean you will get people to follow you. Though Joshua was a leader, his influence was inadequate to overcome the influence of other leaders, which seems to validate the assumption, that varying levels of influence exist within any organization and its integrated chains-of-command. I used the plural here because only a naive leader—or a myopic one—ignores the fact that one of the most fundamental chains-of-command is the informal one that exists in all organizations. It takes a wise and mature leader to know and understand his or her true authority and the limits and capabilities of the control he or she actually exercises.

Another thing of which I am absolutely convinced is that influence can be and often is employed both positively and negatively. While Joshua and Caleb took one position (the affirmative) regarding the invasion of Canaan (and I believe history indicates their view was the right one), ten other leaders took an opposing view (the negative) and prevailed. This indicates clearly that influence cuts like a two-edged sword, leading those who are influenced to follow either to victory or to defeat. This places a great responsibility on leaders to be concerned for the welfare of others, especially their followers.

I have seen countless instances in my lifetime where influence—or rather the power of that influence—has adversely affected the personal motivations of leaders and subsequently similarly impacted the lives of their followers. Joshua and Caleb had a desire to motivate their countrymen toward something that would benefit all of them, and they held steadfastly to that position, even though it was neither popular nor the one that was finally acted upon. Preserving that kind of integrity should be the aspiration of all great leaders. Not compromising on what you feel is right and maintaining that integrity in the face of even insurmountable opposition lays the foundation for organizational and national honor. In the case of Joshua and Caleb, as in many cases today, the prevailing influence of the ten negative and false intelligence reports that were based on the personal fears, ambitions, or desires of those leaders led to an insurrection among the people. There were some who even sought to depose Moses and Aaron and return to Egypt. The result of the misuse of influence for these ten, you will remember, was that they all died of plague and their followers, too, died in the desert. That does not sound like an admirable epitaph to me.

Let's look for a moment at some more reasons for how and why Joshua's influence matured and flourished. I think another reason it grew stronger was his association with the good leadership of Moses. If you want to grow in influence, then seek access to, and accept the mentoring of, other good leaders. By virtue of their acceptance, and inclusion in their circles of influence and tutelage, you will expand your ability to polish your own leadership skills. As you grow, you will inherit the respect of their followers, as we see in **Deuteronomy 31:1–8, 23**.

I also believe that Joshua's influence grew over time, as he became more mature. It is obvious to most scholars that Joshua gave nearly the same speech in **Numbers 14** as he gave in **Joshua 18**, but with completely different results. Why was that? What made the difference? I believe there are multiple reasons. First, he was talking to a completely different generation, a generation that had seen his skills in action grow and his authority become validated; it was a generation that knew of his successful track record. His leadership trait of confidence was also solidifying, and it thus increased the influence Joshua had over people.

Another reason his second speech had a stronger impact was because of the timing. The Israelites had grown tired of wandering and were ready for a change. Understanding the wants and needs of your followers will help you detect the right time to use your influence most effectively, just as Joshua did in **Joshua 1:16–18**.

Joshua's influence also increased because of the impact of his patience and integrity. Even though they were forced to wander for forty years through the wilderness because of a decision over which they had no control and one that was contrary to any decision they would have made, Joshua and Caleb never became cynical, melancholy, angry, or disgruntled. Even though they may have felt they were subjected to an unfair turn of events, they continued to display faithfulness, credibility, consistency, and integrity. As a result, they were the only two leaders to recon the land of Canaan who lived to return there and lead their people to victory, as we learn in **Joshua 1:5–9**.

Finally, I am convinced that Joshua's influence grew because he was right—right in the eyes of God. Standing for what is right is an attribute necessary for any leader and defending what is right in the face of political expediency, popularity, and personal gain is called moral courage. If your motivations and efforts remain true, they will stand the eternal test of time.

In conclusion, while it may be true that leadership is influential, when it comes right down to it, that influence is based primarily on a leader's character, compassion, and the strength of his or her convictions. If you desire to become a leader who can rely on the accomplishments of your followers and not exploit them, then why don't you give your own leadership a 10,000-mile checkup? How do your character, your compassion, and the strength of your convictions and motivations stack up against those of Joshua?

Chapter XIII

Joseph Gained the Gift of Maturity

When we look meticulously into the book of **Genesis 37:1–52**, we will find out that there is a little lesson we can learn about leadership from Joseph. He was a leader who endured trials and reaped rewards, while his leadership and influence matured over time.

Just like money that is wisely invested, which, as time goes by, compounds its value through interest, leaders often increase their own value, stature, and capabilities as time progresses. While all good leaders have some God-given natural abilities, they can all augment their skills through the unfettered nurturing of other leaders. True leadership has many facets, just like a diamond, which need to be perfected over a lifetime—facets like respect, emotional strength, experience, people skills, confidence (not to be confused with arrogance), discipline, vision, momentum, and timing; the list continues, almost ad infinitum, and all these facets need some amount of polishing in order to be brought to their highest potential. We can see, I hope, that all leaders require some amount of seasoning, just like firewood and a fine wine, so I am told.

When looking at his or her life circumspectly, a person can learn just how, over any given period of time, God can work with any one of us to mature our Christian leadership potential. I like to think Joseph was given to us by God as an example of this "Gift of Maturation." I feel that there are four distinct phases of leadership training exemplified in Joseph's journey toward his role as a leader. Before examining these phases, let me first set the stage. Joseph's brothers saw a cocky kid who was not content just to be his father's favorite son; no, they felt like he had to rub his position as the favorite in their faces. When he received a vision from God that he would one day lead his whole family, including his parents and brothers, he enthusiastically told them all about it—not once, but twice. He was rebuked by his father for this perceived arrogance and despised by his brothers, who wanted an inappropriate revenge. Eventually they plotted and executed their plan of deception. Now the stage is set, so let's continue.

In **Phase 1**, which I describe as the "You don't know what you don't know" phase, you can see that Joseph, like most of us, began life in a state of "leadership ignorance." He didn't understand his own family's dynamics, such as how his brothers would react, or maybe he just didn't care what they thought about his vision. It is apparent that Joseph did things and said things without taking into account the impact of his actions on his interpersonal relationships. The result of revealing and claiming his vision was more than two decades of estrangement from his family. A leader who always acts in haste generally harvests less than stellar consequences for themselves and, more often than not, for those around them. Think of the pain caused to Joseph's father, who thought for so long that his beloved son was dead, and the guilt and even remorse that his brothers must have felt when they considered the impact of their actions in response to Joseph's.

In **Phase 2**, which I describe as the "You know what you don't know" phase, Joseph began to understand, during his time in slavery, that there was much about the responsibilities of God's leadership plan for his life that he did not yet understand. He began to feel the weight of leadership. Over those years, he was subject to betrayal and punishment and was also exposed to lessons in human nature and relationship development. It was through these processes that his character began to develop and strengthen, helping him to learn and more fully understand the meaning of humility, patience, and service.

During **Phase 3**, which I will call the "As you know and you grow, it starts to show" phase, Joseph learned that, only after he had paid the price of preparation and learned many of life's lessons the hard way, was he capable of responding to the opportunity promised in his earlier vision and get the chance to display his great skills as a mature leader. His exceptional and wise performance for Pharaoh didn't just happen; he developed his abilities over about thirteen years, paying quite a price. The eventual result, of course, was his promotion to a position of leadership that made him second in command of all Egypt.

In the last stage, **Phase 4**, which I will call the "You simply act because of what you know" phase, you enter the final segment of your leadership journey, a phase that never ends. When Joseph was building storehouses in preparation for the impending famine, he didn't take time to stop to think about what he was learning and how it would benefit him. He simply went about his work daily doing what had to be done to the best of his ability, with all the right motivations, adding to the wealth of his master. And eventually, through the opportunities brought about by his maturation, he was able to fulfill God's vision for his life. This could not happen until the cocky kid who would be the boss became a fully grown and wise leader.

Where are you on the leadership ladder? Are you near the insecure, bossy bottom or climbing toward the more confident, secure, and mature upper end? Wherever you are, remember that leaving a legacy of strong, competent, and ethical leadership is the most effective way there is of positively impacting the future generations to whom we leave the world in which we live.

Chapter XIV

Nehemiah the Navigator

In discussing **Nehemiah 1:1–3; 32**, we are going to review some history on the leadership of Nehemiah, "a man with a plan," as the saying goes, although the US Navy and I have a different way of saying the same thing. Our version goes like this: "Anyone can steer a ship, but it takes a navigator to chart its course."

It seems logical under these circumstances for me to call the leadership principle exemplified by Nehemiah "The Gift of Navigation." High-quality leaders never intentionally navigate by the seat of their pants, as the old proverb states, but rather see the whole course of events in their mind's eye before ever leaving the starting point. Think about Christopher Columbus. First-class leaders can see the destination, needs, obstacles, and who it will take to accomplish the mission before they ever leave the dock, let alone cross the horizon to engage the unknown.

To navigate properly, leaders must balance optimism, reality, intuition, planning, faith, and fact. When leaders plan carefully, they convey confidence and capability. They may make any number of course corrections during the voyage, based on circumstances encountered, but they will not find themselves without a following or the means to succeed. Leaders need to clearly see further than others can toward the eventual solution of any obstacle that may be encountered. Leaders must also be able to anticipate more rapidly than others the support and logistics that the accomplishment of the interim task requires. Good leaders will also realize before others the reasons, justifications, and desired results for the mission.

As an effective leader, you will also need to develop your operational plan and prepare for its execution, so before we go any farther, let's assess Nehemiah's planning process.

Before he did anything else, Nehemiah clearly identified the problem and made it his personal problem. Then he spent time in prayer. I have found that planning anything without consulting higher headquarters is not only foolish but is frequently indicative of an attitude tainted with arrogance—an arrogance often born out of power that so easily infects a leader with the sometimes terminal disease of pride.

Nehemiah then met with the key decision makers of his day regarding his vision. He was wise enough to realize that, without the express and unified support of these critical leaders within his own organization; his efforts would most likely be futile—or, at most, would provide only superficial results. He next assessed both the immediate and the potential future circumstances. After he developed his plan of action (his mission statement), he met with the people and broadcast his vision, encouraging them to participate and calling upon them to take action. When he received their support and agreement, he task organized them and began working toward the accomplishment of their "joint mission." As this mission progressed, he made such adjustments as were necessary to assure its ultimate success.

It should be readily apparent that it takes a "trued" or "boxed" moral and ethical compass to navigate in the turbulent waters of our current society, where even in the church one can find the frequently conflicting winds of fundamentalism, fanaticism, liberalism, legalism, and compromise blowing doctrine about with hurricane force.

One last thing you as a leader must remember always is that it is not the Coxswain who takes the heat for arriving at the wrong target, it's the Navigator and that, mister leader, is you!

Chapter XV

Peter Developed the Ability to Prioritize

In **Acts 6:1–7** there is a lesson we can learn from Peter, a leader who understood that he couldn't do everything there is to do all by himself. Like many of us in the military or law enforcement professions, Peter tended to be a control freak and a micromanager. He was often deluged with more than any one man could be expected to be in charge of, but, through the power of Christ and the wisdom of the Holy Spirit, he was able to organize these tasks and accomplish many great things, primarily through and for the benefit of others. I am sure you law enforcement officers have had those nights on patrol when you asked yourself just who told the dispatcher that you were Superman. You know what I mean: too many calls, not enough time, and three guys called in sick, yet the complainants and your sergeant expect you to handle it.

Peter was wise enough to realize that not everything people want to do necessarily needs to be done. You see, a wise leader must clearly understand that not everything that catches a person's eye should necessarily ignite the passion of his or her heart. A leader's heart and his or her efforts should be focused only on that activity that will result in worthwhile endeavors, the outcome of which will produce accomplishments that truly benefit others and have long-lasting results.

For the purpose of our discussion, we will be referring to this organizational practice of Peter's as "the Gift of Prioritization." Proper utilization of this principle will more often than not help to sharpen a leader's focus by helping him or her concentrate primarily on significant tasks—tasks that will advance the accomplishment of the vision that is shared with their followers. Concentration exercised to the general exclusion of all nonessential activity.

Peter's application of prioritization illustrates a formula that can be mathematically expressed as:

GP + CM = FA *(Great Passion + Clear Mission = Focused Action)*

Go ahead and take a moment to assess your own leadership example, and examine your own understanding and utilization of prioritization. Are your activities spread out all over the place, full of passion but short on direction, or are you focused on the few things that will produce the greatest rewards? Do you finish what you start before going on to another project? Do you try to manage and get involved in every aspect of each task you have going or have delegated? If you are not able to effectively micromanage (which is not really an admirable leadership trait anyway), then delegate the task (which is an admirable quality in a leader) to those you have trained to accomplish that skill and then let them do it, as Peter did when the Grecian Jews came complaining about their physical needs. It was then that Peter realized he could not do all things for all people; as a result, deacons were born into the church and ordained with the appropriate responsibilities and the requisite authority to accomplish their specific mission.

Leaders must concentrate only on what really matters and communicate that attitude to their followers. Prioritization is one of the hardest skills there is for a leader to master because it requires developing the seemingly incongruous ability to tell others, "No." A task not relished by a person with a servant's heart and compassion for those in need.

One of my many military illustrations comes from the WW II US Army logistics operation referred to in history as "The Red Ball Express." Those troops shuttled "Beans, Band-Aids, and Bullets" to the front and wounded warriors to the rear. When asked what they did if convoy vehicles broke down or became battle damaged and blocked the roads, members of the unit would reply, "Haul ass and bypass!" They would qualify that response if the issue was pursued by inquiring of the questioner, "Would you rather receive 80 percent of the supplies or lose 100 percent of the convoy?" Having "faced the elephant" of combat myself on an occasion or two, I know that the answer to that question is obvious.

Now let's look for a moment at the four factors that determined Peter's actions in light of the responsibilities of today's leader.

The **first** thing a leader must do is assess and determine the validity of the need that is brought to him. If the need is found to be essential, he must proceed to the second item.

The **second** thing the leader must do is evaluate the results of deferring or delegating the satisfaction of the need and find out what resources are available.

The **third** thing a leader must do is determine what leadership opportunities may exist in satisfying the need. Is it possible to use the process of satisfying this need to further the confidence, the technical proficiency, or the visibility and viability of some of your subordinate leaders? If so, that alone might increase its priority. As a leader, you must never forget that your primary responsibility is to serve and develop your subordinates.

The **fourth** thing a leader must be able to do is delegate lower-priority tasks to competent subordinates for the utmost efficiency of the organization and for their own professional development. This process increases your efficiency and increases their overall value to both the organization and themselves. But always make sure you know your people's skills and their limitations.

No matter what the outcome, you can never and should never even attempt to divert any of the responsibility from yourself. You should instead focus on publicly and professionally commissioning, commending, and recognizing those subordinates you have empowered to accomplish specific and integral tasks necessary for the joint success of your mission. This public confirmation of their abilities will serve to strengthen the bonds of leadership in all directions. Sadly, this confirmation and recognition is often sacrificed by current-day leaders, who appear to be more achievement-driven rather than character-driven.

Never forget that most people spend 80 percent of their time on 20 percent of their taskings, because they fail to recognize the efficiency of teamwork and fail to exhibit the faith they say they have in their subordinates. That characteristic is more indicative of power than of leadership.

Chapter XVI

Moses and Joshua and the Gift of Mentoring

As we venture into **Numbers 27:18–23** for our next lesson, we will be learning from the lives of Moses and Joshua, whom I sometimes classify as mentoring leaders. This is a leadership lesson about leaders who train others to become leaders.

I am sure you have heard that old cliché, "It takes one to know one!" You can hear that phrase screamed by kids on playgrounds all across the English-speaking world. Or how about the saying "You've seen one, you've seen them all." Both of these sayings reflect a shared bond between members of like identities. That identity bond goes a little farther when discussing mentoring. I learned long ago that being a mentor is like being a teacher. I also learned that there are predominantly two types of people in this world, teachers and learners and the best teachers are life-long learners. Thus, it seems logical to me that with the help of good mentors, some learners will mature into good mentors themselves.

Moses realized something we have already mentioned, but it deserves to be repeated often, especially to leaders who are legends in their own minds. Moses' realization was that he, like all leaders, both good and bad, would not live forever, and a new leader would eventually be required to take his place. He also knew that if he wanted that new leader to carry on the vision and work God had given him, he needed to find and train a leader after his own heart. The leader to be whom he began training was Joshua.

For simplicity's sake, we will call this "The Gift of Mentoring." For a person's vision and leadership to continue into the next generation, they must be willingly passed along and willingly received. Moses seamlessly passed along his leadership responsibilities to Joshua during the many years they spent together. He did not just drop these responsibilities on him all at once. Instead, as Joshua matured and was deemed ready, Moses gradually allowed him to exercise and develop new responsibilities, using his own leadership style, while still studying under his (Moses') supervision.

Moses began by vesting some of his own authority in Joshua, thus empowering him. He did this with a public commissioning and by publicly displaying his own acceptance, approval, and recognition of Joshua and his leadership. Moses knew that, after this public expression of faith, nobody would question the fact that Joshua was one of Moses' leaders. When you publicly display the courage to vest your own authority in others, commensurate with the responsibilities you delegate to them, you express the same level of faith and trust in those future leaders that Moses showed with Joshua. You will thus reinforce their image in the eyes of those they also lead. Once you empower them, you need to move to the background and let them lead. Remain close at hand for the times they will need your advice and support, but let them lead while you are still around to help them when they falter or outright fail. Never forget that we never really learn from success, since we apparently already knew how to accomplish the task. We should, however, always learn from our failures. Therefore, you must follow the failure of your subordinate leaders with evaluation, instruction, exhortation, and an expression of your continued support. Isn't this the technique we use to raise our children? We allow them to slowly extend their wings until they are capable of flying on their own.

As Joshua matured and gained experience as a leader, Moses looked for opportunities for Joshua to apply what he had learned. Moses did not merely allow Joshua to watch; he allowed him to participate in the leading of Israel so he could experience all the facets of being a leader— both the anticipated highs and the inevitable lows. Joshua performed duties as a military commander, a spy, and as Moses' personal assistant during the developmental stages of his career. Most of all, he was a wise, honest, loyal, and qualified follower who learned to be a leader.

During his training, encouragement and affirmation were never far away. Moses allowed Joshua to learn by maintaining close contact, sharing his time, and not allowing Joshua to be unduly criticized for mistakes either of them might make. He did this while still allowing—in fact, even encouraging—Joshua to exercise his own independent judgment and developing style of leadership. By providing appropriate encouragement and validating his confidence in Joshua as the future leader of the Israelites, Moses fostered a relationship with him that provided for the continuity of leadership that would be needed to further God's plan.

Joshua is a great example of any future generation of leaders in that, while he may have had a modicum of confidence, he still needed to mature. So let's take a look at what future leaders really need to accomplish in order to be prepared to lead.

From themselves they will need conviction, courage (both physical and moral), and obedience, since these are the cornerstones of a good leader's character. These they will need to find within themselves, and such qualities will come readily if they maintain their faith in God.

Their mentor will need to equip them like a parent equips a child, so I'll drop the word PARENT on you as another acronym that might help point you toward just what I think it takes to form a good mentor-subordinate relationship.

The *P* stands for **Purpose**. This refers to the mentor/leader's vision for the future. It stands to reason that, if you want someone to carry your dream on, you will have to share it with them clearly and help them adopt that vision as their own. If you are not able to make that connection, your dream will grow old and die along with you.

The *A* stands for **Assessment**. Honest and supportive evaluations are always required for anyone to experience growth. Honest feedback does not always have to take on the vile image of criticism. There is a saying I learned a long time ago in the Marine Corps that still bears a lot of truth. I have seen it validated time and time again during my lifetime. It is short and to the point and goes like this: "Any fool can criticize and most fools do!" Evaluations and honest assessments are essential to any leader's growth and should always be provided with appropriate compassion, since they are in reality both the fruits of experience and knowledge, and the seeds of wisdom. Your subordinates, like your children, are depending on you for the legacy your knowledge and experience (wisdom) will provide.

The *R* stands for **Relationship**. Relationships are the glue that bind us all together. You and those you lead will never be truly successful without a strong personal relationship. The greater the challenges you face together, the greater the growth and strength of the future leader. The relationship you develop will also directly affect the degree of joint ownership that emerges regarding the vision you desire to pass along.

The *E* stands for **Encouragement**. Encouragement is a remarkable weapon against defeat; it may be the only thing you have to instill perseverance in a future leader. Use it wisely and frequently, but not inappropriately. Commending undeserving actions reduces the stature of the giver and reinforces the inappropriate actions of the receiver, while disheartening observers. Still, in the hour of failure, never forget that the only person who never makes a mistake is a person who never takes a risk, and that means that he or she is person who never goes anywhere or grows in value.

The *N* stands for **Navigation**. This is a hands-on skill. Never forget that, while you are mentoring a subordinate in the fine art of navigation, you are still the navigator, directing everyone toward the final destination. Arriving at the targeted destination is always your responsibility as long as you are the primary leader. Remember that US Navy saying we learned a chapter or two back, the one that goes something like this: "Anyone can steer a ship, but it takes a navigator to plot the course." I guarantee you, you will find no shortage of folks willing to steer your ship, but far fewer who are qualified to navigate that vessel safely into the future. If you fail to instruct others in the requirements and skills necessary to do your job and lead, then both the leadership and future of your dream will flounder on the rocks and shoals of life.

Last, but not least, the *T* stands for **Training**. Everyone needs help in developing the skill sets and tools they will need to use in life. Teach them with the same compassion and understanding that parents display when teaching their children. Exercise good judgment, a finely honed sense of timing mixed with patience, perspective, and a positive attitude. When it is necessary to apply discipline, remember that that word means training, not punishment.

It is really from God that future leaders must find validation for the vision with which they are endowed. As these leaders grow and develop their own visions, so, too, will your vision evolve through them. However, your vision may grow even stronger after you are merely a footnote in history. As it develops a life of its own, it will eventually cease being your vision and become one that God has placed on the heart of a new leader.

Finally, from those they serve, the emerging leader needs to encourage support. Without the support of those we serve, neither we nor any leader we train will ever amount to a hill of beans. It has been said that no man is an island; that the actions of everyone have an effect on someone else. And as the maxim goes, we all are actors on the world's stage, and we all have a part to play, and that includes those being served. For, you see, it is into those masses that our new leader will delve to find the next generation's leaders. One final thought to you leaders: without loyal followers there is no—absolutely no—need for leaders.

Chapter XVII

Paul Saw the Need for Reproduction

If you take a careful and studious look at **II Timothy 2:1**, you can learn quite a bit about the man called Paul. You will find that he was a leader who believed in training and preparing others to become leaders. It should become quite clear, as you get into his life, that Paul understood that when you only train followers, the growth and progress toward the acquisition and implementation of your vision and goals can only be gradually achieved because only one person at a time is receiving the message of that dream and continuing to carry it on toward fruition. Apparently Paul believed, as do I, that when you train multiple leaders, the progress toward the culmination of that vision is increased exponentially. This occurs because you harness the efforts and followers of each leader you train and infect them with the significance of your mission. The benefit of training numerous leaders and not just gathering followers can easily be compared to the difference between addition and multiplication. So let's take the time to compare some of the differences between the two types of leaders—those who have, and those who don't have, what I will refer to as "The Gift of Reproduction." I hope to be able to show you just what some of the differences are between leaders who gather followers (for the satisfaction of their own egos) and leaders who train leaders (for the benefit of their mission and future generations).

Leaders who train followers usually need to be needed. They are often in need of what psychologists refer to as ego stroking. Leaders of this nature will always gather at least a small number of followers; however, they will rarely be well equipped enough to prepare those followers ever to undertake any leadership responsibilities on their own. These leaders are often insecure in their own right and will unintentionally pass that inadequacy on to those they train. They will typically make an effort to hide that insecurity behind a facade of false bravado. They will also frequently display that most disruptive of characteristics, which their subordinates recognize as micromanagement.

Quite the opposite is true of leaders who train others to become leaders themselves. These kinds of leaders always want to succeed. They are far more interested, however, in being succeeded. They are less apt to be interested in gathering a following of their own than they are in leaving future generations a legacy of leaders capable of leading and continuing the life of a vision, mission, or goal toward a victorious conclusion. Their passing into history is marked solely by transition and not by the self-construction of temporal or worldly monuments to their achievements, because their achievements are living and breathing and continuing to train another generation of leaders. Leaders like these will never be forgotten by those whom they have led, and will in fact, in some small way, always be a part of those they have trained.

Right here is a good place to remind you, once again, that the greatest of our leaders are not measured by what they themselves achieve—résumés terminate with your earthly demise—but by the things they achieve for and through others.

Another thing about leaders who gather followers is that they tend to focus on people's weaknesses because this makes them feel superior and more secure and qualified in their positions. It does nothing, however, to strengthen or help their subordinates reach the pinnacle of their own leadership potential. Leaders of this type use the weaknesses of others to gain or sustain their sense of their own superiority. They focus almost exclusively on their own priorities, placing them far above all else.

Thankfully, though, there are still leaders who possess a strong and overriding desire to train others to be leaders. These people focus on developing their subordinates' strengths and reducing their weaknesses because that is the key to developing the potential of any future leader. Leaders like these are never afraid to train themselves out of a job. They realize that the future never belongs to the current generation; it is and always will remain a mystery that can only be unlocked and understood by those reaching it. Providing the future with strong, capable, and dedicated leaders who will continue to develop others to carry on this tradition of excellence—a tradition and training they themselves received from past leaders who have taken their rightful places in the annals of history—is their ultimate goal.

It seems to me that those leaders who primarily focus on gathering followers will find themselves time and again dealing with the problems of the bottom 20 percent of their entourage. This faction is often the loudest, most complaining, and least productive segment of their following. Still, they require the most maintenance and will frequently require the disproportionate diversion of precious resources, causing an elevated overall reduction in the efficiency of the entire group.

By contrast, when you study the kinds of leaders who direct their efforts with clear motives and insight, it becomes obvious that those leaders who focus on building future leaders will target the top 20 percent of their staff. Studies show that these are the ones who almost always produce more than is required of them. Focusing on this block of potential leaders not only increases an organization's efficiency and productivity but also allows the potential of these future leaders to be unleashed, tested, refined, and validated under the guidance of tried and tested leaders. This process develops a broad base of qualified leadership simply waiting to be tapped as both current and future needs dictate.

Leaders who gather followers may also look at everyone as having the same capabilities because they lack the capability to recognize and intricately employ the interlocking strengths and weaknesses that each person may possess. These critical strengths and weaknesses when employed properly can often prove to be very beneficial toward the successful accomplishment of the leader's mission. Ignoring them may result in disastrous consequences.

While in contrast to the above category of leader, leaders who are always on the lookout for ways to develop others as leaders recognize that each person is an individual. They can see the strengths and weaknesses of each person and know just how to integrate their complementary capabilities into an efficient and productive workforce. When Paul went on his missionary journeys, he didn't take along just anyone who wanted to go; he selected his companions wisely according to their capabilities, calling, and willingness to serve. That, my friend, is a proven formula for success.

Leaders who work to gather followers seem to be spending most of their time focusing on people in their immediate circumstances. Leaders who build leaders are really investing their time not only in people as they are, but in the people they will become in the future. For example, Paul saw little reason to spend time on John Mark during the time frame of **Acts 13:13** and was therefore reluctant to do so, as discussed in **Acts 15:37–40**. However, with Paul's blessing, Barnabas, another of Paul's leadership team members, invested his time working directly with John Mark. This allowed Paul to direct his efforts toward Timothy, a potential leader who was by now ready for increased responsibilities, and two valuable assets were thus produced for the future good of Paul's mission.

One last thing I have noticed about leaders who gather followers is that they ask for very little commitment, whereas leaders who train leaders ask for and require a great deal of dedication. When you ask people merely to follow, there is very little commitment involved on their part except for recognizing the responsibility for their own actions. When you ask people to lead, however, they must accept the responsibility not only for themselves, but for the welfare of others and for the consequences of their actions as well. There is also the increased requirement for personal sacrifice.

Paul knew and understood something that it would be wise for anyone who desires to be a good leader never to forget—that those leaders who gather followers will at best impact the present, while leaders who train leaders will not only impact the present, but will have a marked impact on the future of generations yet to come.

To be a good mentor of future leaders requires that you never forget you maintain an obligation to keep learning yourself. While it may be true that a good leader can gather a band of followers and achieve a worthy goal, it is only a great leader who can gather, prepare, and direct a band of leaders toward the achievement of as yet uncharted goals.

As we bring this lesson to a conclusion, think back to what I said in the beginning. I remember being told somewhere along life's highway that there are only two types of people you will meet along the way—those people who are teachers and those who are learners. *I have since learned from experience that the best teachers nearly always come from the latter group.*

Chapter XVIII

Esther Had a Sense of Timing

This may sound a bit out of character for a leader, but part of leading and leading well is knowing and understanding when to lead and when not to lead. So let's look at a leader who came to really understand that concept, shall we? Our next lesson in leadership will come from **Esther 4:6–17**.

First, however, I may need to refresh your memory about just who Esther was. Esther is recorded in the Bible as being a woman of deep faith, courage, and patriotism. She was ultimately willing to risk her life for her adoptive father, Mordecai, and for the Jewish people. In her time, women no matter what their status rarely became involved in matters of state. Esther followed her convictions and took the leader's role when it was thrust upon her. Scripture portrays her as a woman raised up as an instrument in the hand of God to avert the destruction of the Jewish people, and to afford them protection and promote their wealth and peace during their captivity.

Four years after Queen Vashti was executed, King Ahasuerus chose Esther to be his wife and queen. Esther was recommended for this role by Mordecai, her cousin and guardian. Shortly after Esther became queen, Mordecai overheard a plot to assassinate the king. He promptly told Esther, who warned her husband of the threat even though that act alone opened both her uncle and herself up to potentially dangerous consequences. An investigation was carried out, and the conspirators were swiftly arrested and executed. The king ordered Mordecai's deed recorded in history. Now let's move into our lesson.

Shall we start by looking at why Esther is considered an Old Testament leader who not only knew how to lead but also knew when to lead? Knowing when to take action and lead is always as important as knowing what to do and where you are going. Winston Churchill once said, "There comes a special moment in everyone's life, a moment for which that person was truly born ... that special opportunity, when he seizes it ... will be his finest hour."

So I will call Esther's contribution to our study of leadership "The Gift of Timing." If you want to be an effective leader, your sense of timing will need to be honed to a razor's edge, as it may often prove to be the critical factor in achieving the successful completion of your mission or vision. Being able to read the handwriting on the wall, as the saying goes, and knowing just what to do may not always prove to be enough. Sometimes only the right action applied at exactly the right time will produce the desired outcome; anything else will be disastrous and will extract too high a price from those involved. Let's look at some things that might happen if you fail to act in accordance with the dictates of this lesson.

First, you need to remember that win, lose, or draw, your fate, as the commander, will be the same as that of your subordinate leaders and followers. We sometimes forget—or completely fail to realize—that when armies lose battles and wars, so do their generals. Leaders are always as affected by the risks they take as are those who follow them. Mordecai needed to remind Esther of that fact. Even though she was a queen, she would still have fared no better than the rest of the Jews if she hadn't acted and spoken with the king at precisely the appropriate time.

Another thing to keep in mind is that any leader who fails to respond to God's timely calling can be replaced by Him with someone else. Mordecai reminded Esther that God would accomplish his purposes with or without her involvement. A leader's willingness to act when God speaks is always a key factor, so be sure whom you're listening to, and don't always use the "I'll pray about it" cliché as a way of putting off your decision. How would you feel if, every time you told your son to take out the trash, wash the car or the dishes, mow the lawn, or do his homework, he responded with "I need time to pray about it"? Remember partial obedience is more properly spelled "DISOBEDIENCE."

If you fail to respond within a proper time period, you could lose more than just an opportunity. I have frequently heard people say that a wrong decision beats no decision, and sometimes that may in fact be true. But making the right decision at the right time, though it may seem to be risky, will certainly avoid the greater risk of merely standing by and accepting the consequences, which, I might add, are often the same for making no decision as they are for making a wrong decision. The difference is usually measured in your display of courage under fire and your willingness to accept the responsibility for your actions, not your inaction.

Poor timing might also cause you to miss out on your real mission in life. Churchill also once said that that key moment in your life that he spoke of is a fleeting one; God will still use you, but will he ever use you as effectively as he might have if you had grown that little bit more during your prime opportunity? You need always to keep in mind that the fear of taking risks does not come from God; the peace and strength to make tough decisions does. Remember, it is Satan and not Christ who wants you to bear the weight of fear and guilt. Through Christ, God removed your guilt and shame, once and for all, at Calvary. When you feel the burden of fear, guilt, or sin pressing down on you, turn your thoughts to the one who removed all those burdens on the cross and, as he directed all of us to do, "cast your cares upon him all ye who are heavy laden." Leadership is often a lonely task, but it is something that you need not shoulder alone.

Avoiding decisions because of their difficulty or high risk factor will never solve your dilemma. You will only succeed and grow as a leader by making one timely decision after another. There is not now, nor will there ever be, such a thing as a zero risk decision, especially for a person in a position of leadership. It is a time-tested, proven fact that your successful decisions will eventually have a compounding effect on your confidence, and they will build on each other as they reinforce another leadership principle called momentum.

Now let me give you five tests of timing you can use as a reference when you are faced with any decision-making opportunity.

First, consider the real needs that exist around you. Keep a clear picture of what your followers actually need and what they think they need and expect from you, and remember that a man's perception is always reality for him. Always try to be aware of the mood, vision, and capabilities of your subordinate leaders and their followers. Keeping a close watch on the mission, manpower, motivation, and morale of your unit or organization will ensure that you are more prepared to face the decision-making process than the leader who ignores such critical factors. You also need to remember that if you are leading properly, there are layers of leadership that must be considered. You exercise your leadership over a following of leaders while those budding leaders lead theirs.

Your **second** consideration should be the prioritization of the opportunities that exist before you. Georgia farmers will tell you that all the peaches on the tree don't ripen at the same time. Keep your eyes open for the appropriate opportunity, and act when that peach begins to blush. The helter-skelter or "up to my butt in alligators" approach of tackling too many opportunities at one time is guaranteed to result in none of the projects being accomplished in an appropriate or timely manner.

A **third** consideration regarding timing must be the things that are influencing you to act. You always need to test your motivation, since it can be quite easily corrupted by power, popularity, notoriety, and success, so rely on the trusted inner circle of wise and competent staff advisors that you have chosen, trained, and matured. They should not be expected to make the decisions for you but to provide you with sage advice and additional points of view. Feedback and perspective are always essential ingredients in any recipe for success.

Your **fourth** consideration must be your past successes. Experience and knowledge really are a great team of instructors. While you are building a reputation through your successful achievements, knowledge and experience are growing right along with you. As your leadership improves, you will in due course be the one sought after for advice, just as the king eventually sought out Esther for advice. Why does this phenomenon occur? I think it is due to the growing realization that gained experience or acquired knowledge alone are nowhere near as effective independently as they are when the reservoirs of both are emptied into the same raging river called wisdom.

The **fifth** thing to consider is your own courage. You must have both the physical and moral courage to act, and that will require you to risk and to reach. You must, if you are to become a leader, reach beyond your fears and risk many things for the sake of others. This will be an extremely difficult assignment unless you have real compassion and a heartfelt desire to lead.

Esther demonstrated her ability to act with courage and in a timely manner, even though she was troubled by fear and hesitation. With God's help, she stepped forward in spite of her doubts and was recorded as a biblical leader with qualities worthy of emulation.

Before moving on, you might want to take time to reread the Old Testament Book of Esther and put yourself in her place. Would you have answered the challenge as she did, or would you have tried to learn to swim on the beach?

Chapter XIX

Solomon Exemplified Momentum

Our lesson this time will come from the book of **I Kings 2:1**, where we can learn more about leadership from King Solomon, who was a leader who did not just make things happen but kept them happening.

Momentum is critical for successful leaders because it is a dynamic force that creates a life of its own. Followers can become infected with it and managers can strive to control it, but it takes sound leaders to create it. There is an old adage most of us know that states, "If you can't stand the heat, get out of the kitchen." You have more than likely heard that saying many times before, but now you are going to learn that it has a close military relative in the leadership field. That relative adage goes like this: "If you can't *make* some heat, then get out of the kitchen." You see, Solomon, like all good ship captains, realized that "you can't steer a ship unless it is moving." A stationary vessel will never reach its destination, and a leader who cannot initiate momentum will never accomplish very much, either.

Growth and change are inextricably linked and can never be separated; both bring into play the leadership "Gift of Momentum," which Solomon utilized so effectively. Momentum is a key element of a successful leader's credentials. Without momentum, even the smallest obstacles or inconveniences will seem insurmountable. With enough momentum, however, nearly any complication or barrier can be overcome. So let's take a look at how Solomon took the momentum he received from his father King David and sustained and perpetuated that momentum, using it to ultimately accomplish the changes that made him the distinguished leader he finally became.

Solomon began his reign as a leader solely with what his father David provided. He was left a stable kingdom, plenty of resources, wise counsel, and, above all, a public endorsement of his leadership. Israel knew beyond any shadow of a doubt that it had a leader in Solomon.

When Solomon began his leadership journey as a young man, he humbly asked God for wisdom—a trait he regarded as a leadership necessity above all else. When he asked God for wisdom, he did so recognizing his position, his responsibilities, and the potential difficulties and sacrifices he would face on his quest to become a great leader. Solomon knew in his heart he would need wisdom above all other things. So he asked God to provide him with an understanding heart—one that would keep his motives pure in judging God's people. Not a bad decision for an eighteen-year-old, was it?

During his reign, Solomon made many wise decisions that won for him widespread credibility. His wise decisions affecting both internal and external matters placed him in high standing among the people. His legendary decision regarding the parentage of a baby won the respect of all who heard about it, and people came from far and near to learn or benefit from his God-given talents.

During his reign, he maintained peace and harmony throughout the land. He was able to avert a bloody civil war and took wise precautions to avert attack from other nations, thereby maintaining peace on every side. (**I Kings 4:24**)

Solomon surrounded himself with a wise military and administrative staff. While it is true that he selected only a few of David's wise counselors (which, in and of itself, may have been the product of wisdom), he added other wise leaders whom he himself had nurtured. He thus surrounded himself with both loyalty and competence. He not only sustained the momentum inherited from David, his father and predecessor, but also augmented it by exhibiting a willingness to accept an overall responsibility for perpetuating that momentum. It seems that some leaders are only willing to accept that responsibility when the momentum is rolling along, producing success after success. Great leaders, though, must accept the responsibility for slowdowns much more readily than they will accept the accolades for uninterrupted success. It is generally regarded as sound management when, after three years of leadership in any great organization, every success and every setback experienced by the organization is perceived to be the leader's responsibility.

Solomon was also good at directing momentum and not letting it direct him. He received the reins of leadership from his father, David, a great warrior king and an outstanding military tactician. Solomon, however, was a king who led Israel with an emphasis not on combat and conflict but on trade and construction. This required a redirection in the momentum that he received from David, a change Solomon was willing and able to foster. I want to remind you that a more modern-day leader—Thomas Jefferson—once said regarding change, "In matters of fashion, go with the flow, but, in matters of conscience, stand as firm as a rock." I see that as reinforcing the concept of being willing to take the road less traveled if you truly believe it is the right road.

I am sure that Solomon, like most leaders, probably had to work at maintaining his enthusiasm, especially during difficult times. Leaders must always strive to remain positive in the face of disaster, and great leaders must show great amounts of enthusiasm. They must believe and make others believe, as Solomon could, that the work they are doing is the most important work they could be doing, and that it really matters. You see, I have found that a sense of purpose fuels enthusiasm, which produces momentum.

Leaders like Solomon must also be able to convey the idea that the people they are working with are the best and will give their very best every time; therefore I, their leader, must always give my best in support of them.

When you can accomplish these tasks, the results will generally be positive. Good leaders will rarely be surprised; they know they will get the kind of results they expect. Conversely, poor leaders with a defeatist attitude who fail to develop and maintain their unit or organization's momentum will also get what they anticipate and will likely look for someone else to blame.

Chapter XX

King David's Gift of Accountability

Personal accountability is a leadership lesson that can never be over-looked, so we are going to dive into **I Chronicles 11:10–12:40** and learn something, I hope, about the importance of seeking and listening to wise counsel from David, who was a leader known to many by the company he kept. When you take time to study the life of King David, you will find that he was a great warrior and an intelligent leader, though obviously not always a perfect one. (Are any of us perfect?) David did, however, surround himself predominantly with wise lead-ers and loyal and dedicated men of character, allowing them to hold him accountable for his actions. He was well aware that there is no place for lone rangers in the world of leadership. The staff with which a leader chooses to encircle himself frequently determines whether or not he will be able to realize his ultimate potential. A strong leader who chooses a weak and pandering staff comprised predominantly of yes-men can never truly expect to make a lasting impact. Conversely, even a mediocre leader who is willing to select a strong group of com-petent leaders for his staff and closest advisors and allow them to lead will experience an excellent chance of moving his vision for the future forward a significant distance.

It seemed obvious to me as I conducted my study of his life that David possessed what can be referred to as a "Gift of Personal Accountability" to a greater extent than many leaders of whom we have spoken thus far in our study, and far beyond the degree exemplified by Sampson.

David was wise enough to start building his staff of trusted and com-petent leaders long before he became king. In **I Chronicles** and in

I Samuel, for example, we learn that many strong warriors were attracted to David's side during his rise up the often treacherous slopes of the leadership pyramid. And he didn't attract just anyone; he attracted people who wanted to be leaders themselves. He also chose from those recruits wisely, selecting men with varying gifts—ambidextrous archers, slingers, spearmen, mighty men of valor, and hundreds of captains. David, you see, knew how to diversify his assets, thus solidifying his command and preparing it for most emergencies.

The loyalty of David's leaders was appropriately reflected in the loyalty of his men. David had his ups and downs, just like every one who walks the leadership road, and he felt the entire spectrum of emotional warfare, but he realized that he never walked that trail alone; God saw that David's concerns were for others and blessed his followers. From the earliest days through the toughest times, even when it looked as if David's own son Absalom would crush his father, many of David's followers steadfastly maintained their loyalty, remaining by his side. This was in part because of the style of leadership David embraced; he was a leader who delegated and did not feel as though he had to do it all. This provided his developing leaders with a chance to grow into their own competency and reach leadership maturity. We must acknowledge that this display of confidence can never be undertaken without risk. Still, strong leaders are—and must always be—willing to take great but calculated risks not just take risks.

It is a fact, though, that even good leaders can err, and this is exemplified by David, who was an "adulterer, and murderer" or as some see him a coconspirator in an ancient homicide. But don't forget: he was also called a man after God's own heart. He was well aware of what it felt like to be close to God and therefore recognized when he had separated himself from God by his self-serving actions. David, however, understood what it was necessary to do in order to return to the shelter and peace of God when separated from Him by sin. He was always willing to be held accountable for his sin when it was presented to him and to repent of it. David is an excellent example of God using a man who saw great highs and great lows in his life but who never lost sight of God and was rewarded by being recognized as a part of the lineage of Christ.

But what did David look for in the members of his command staff and advisors, and what should we look for as we select our own subordinate leaders? Let's take a look at some of the qualities that make up a strong leader's immediate subordinates—or what some of them may refer to as their INNER CIRCLE. That looks like a good acronym, so let's stick with it and break it down as we look at what it takes to make up a wise council of commanders.

Making **Influential** people a part of your staff usually compounds your own influence. Always remember that those people over whom you have some degree of influence exercise some degree of influence over others. As this net spreads, a leader's influence increases exponentially. The influence of these subordinates must constantly be monitored and channeled for the good of the many and should never be allowed to become competitive with the influence of the overall leadership steering the mission and its leader's vision.

Including people on your staff who are good at **Networking** generally expands the resources available to accomplish any mission you may select or be assigned. People who know other people have more resources to bring to bear on solving a wider variety of problems.

Placing **Nurturing** people close to you will help remind you to keep your focus on others, because this sort of person is the type who cares about others and will focus on caring for, encouraging, and supporting them. This display of compassion rarely adversely impacts a leader's reputation; instead, it usually amplifies that reputation.

Empowering people must be included because they have the ability, confidence, and understanding to ensure the implementation of that empowerment principle at lower levels. These are the people who will find ways to help you accomplish more because they are confident, competent achievers themselves and know how to lead and empower others.

Introducing **Resourceful** people to your staff is critical because these are the kind of people who can think and act on their own without selfish motives; they are always a boon to any organization. These staff members can think on their feet, as the saying goes, and they possess the ability to engage any obstacle on the fly and then to improvise, adapt, and overcome these obstacles they encounter, while continuing to advance the leader's vision.

Character-driven people are people of strong character and should always be included on a command staff because they will help polish a leader's integrity, keeping that leader honest and allowing him or her to accomplish much more than those of questionable character. You see, having a staff laden with individuals of weak character will inevitably distort any leader's moral compass and destroy that leader's reputation, dashing any prospects of future success. A leader needs to view their word and the word of his or her staff members as the seed of their nation's honor.

Intuitive people are those who not only can, but do, use their God-given instincts to anticipate what actions will be required and when they will be necessary, in order to head off potential problems. These staffers make quite competent strategic planners and are therefore very valuable contributors to any leader's staff.

Putting **Responsible** people on your staff means you will have included people who will never leave you in the lurch. These are men and women of their word—men and women who don't generate excuses or look for places to stack blame. If you are going to empower staffers, then you need them to be responsible people. Authority without responsibility is a dog that eventually attacks its master.

Don't forget **Competent** people. You don't need a staff of world-class performers, but you do need skillful people who can and do desire to inspire others. Competence, by its very nature, breeds competence. And that means that incompetence tends to breed incompetence, so when you must relieve and replace incompetent leaders, never replace them with a member of their own staff. It pays to realize that your followers cannot see luck, but they can see performance, perseverance, and proficiency.

Loyal people are a mandate, as trust is a compulsory obligation. Without it, the rest of these staff qualities are meaningless. It has been pointed out by many people familiar with good leadership that "any fool can criticize and most fools do". Disloyal and therefore deceitful subordinates will eventually and without doubt destroy anything they encounter, especially unit morale. A lack of loyalty in a unit generally means that everyone is looking for a place to lay the blame for failure, rather than concentrating on reaching a successful conclusion to their mission. That type of organization can more appropriately be called a mob. You always need to remember the loyalty of Brutus.

Energetic people are always part of a successful staff. Energetic people are tenacious people—the kind of people for whom the encountering of failure after minor failure is viewed only as opportunity for growth. These are people who just won't let themselves be sidetracked. Wars would always go to the winner of the first battle if it weren't for the persistent and energetic efforts of warriors and wise commanders who seize the opportunities provided by adversity to learn from each and every mistake to improvise, adapt, and overcome. It is wise to remember that, without adversity, courage never blossoms.

Look around and you will see the kind of people God can and will provide to support you in your leadership quest. You still have to put together the team He gives you and use it according to the vision He has instilled in your heart and mind. Thus, in conclusion, I remind you that if you surround yourself with eagles, you will soar to victory, but if you surround yourself with turkeys, you are likely to end up being the guest of honor on someone's Thanksgiving table.

Chapter XXI

David and Saul Had Different Views on Personal Boundaries

Do you know what it is that keeps a person from reaching his or her full potential? There are many things that can distract, hinder or block the still-maturing leader. From **II Samuel 5:1–4**, from the team of David and Saul, we are going to gain some knowledge about one of those things; something called dealing with personal limitations. David and Saul were both kings whose leadership abilities and personal views of leadership determined their ultimate effectiveness. We are going to find out that these two kings held very different perspectives on what they felt they could and could not do. I know from experience that a person can let their professional and socially perceived boundaries put a man-hole cover on their dreams, whereas others only let these expectations provide them with an opportunity to take that often "self-imposed" manhole cover and turn it into a Frisbee.

Most of us undoubtedly know that King David and King Saul were historical leaders of the Israelite nation, but what was it that made them two such different people? The answer, I believe, lies in their different abilities to understand and properly utilize the leadership gifts with which God empowered them.

It has often been said that individuals only rise to the highest level of their own incompetence and there they remain. (This is known as the Peter Principle). I have another version that I subscribe to, and it goes like this: "individuals rise to the highest level of their own perceived competence" (the Fairman Principle). The Peter Principle might seem to indicate that most leaders reach a level where they become incompetent and thus stagnant. Perish that thought, amigo! Real leaders will lift the bar, lid, or ceiling of limitations wherever, whenever, and however they encounter one. Doing that requires leadership ability. That ability allows them to force up even the most difficult and restrictive lids that the world ostensibly wants to screw down so tightly on their jar of life.

For a few minutes, we are going to scrutinize their, David and Saul's, lives and see just what made David succeed where Saul failed. We'll call this lesson "the Gift of Personal Boundaries." As we proceed, we will find out that David routinely exceeded his perceived limitations, while Saul never came close to fully realizing his own capabilities.

Let's look first at some of the similarities in these two men's lives, shall we? Both of them received counsel from God. Saul received his through Samuel, David through Samuel and later, during his reign as king, from Nathan. Samuel anointed both as chosen by God to be kings. They shared similar and great challenges, including the challenge of facing Goliath. But let's look more closely at their differing responses. Saul, a tried and proven great warrior, hid in fear from Goliath and the Philistines, whereas David, a mere shepherd boy, responded with courage and honor to the obnoxious Goliath's blasphemy. Later on in their lives, both of them, when confronted with their shortcomings, had an opportunity to repent of their inappropriate activities and to change or not to change when confronted with these shortcomings. Saul chose to speak not a whisper of repentance nor to express any appropriate sorrow over his unauthorized burnt offering and later consultation with the witch of Endor. David, however, felt extreme remorse and responded to his guilt by breaking down and repenting when confronted by Nathan regarding his sordid affair with Bathsheba and his subsequent involvement in the death of her husband, Uriah.

Next, let's concentrate on Saul for a minute or two and see if you can recognize some perceived barriers in your own life, based on obstacles he confronted in his life. Let's also see if you can learn to deal with them by examining how he dealt with his boundaries.

First, there was fear. Fear exists in all of us, but it was not put there by God. Fear comes from the devil, whereas from God comes the spirit of courage. Remember, though, that, without fear, courage can never materialize, and, without adversity, it will never blossom. When faced by Goliath of the Philistines, Saul succumbed to his fears and was found hiding among the equipment, when he should have remained faithful to God and never allowed his fear to surpass his faith. (if I remember This also happened to Peter with regard to Jesus' arrest, but, unlike Saul, Peter felt remorse and repented. Saul also had a problem with impatience. When he refused to wait for Samuel as he had been directed and offered an illegal sacrifice, he assumed privileges that God had not intended for him, and, as a result, he suffered some dire consequences.

Playing God is never a good idea, though in both my career as a US Marine and my career as a law enforcement officer, I have often observed that role being played by some of my brothers and sisters in arms. Not very well, I might add. It also pays to remember, when you are in a hurry, that Christ advised us that those who would be first will often end up last.

Another problem Saul dealt with was his inability to accept the facts as they were presented to him. He refused to relinquish his reign after Samuel told him God had rejected him as king. Killing the messenger never changes the message. At best, it delays validation of the message but never changes the consequences of ignoring it. Saul was impulsive, as well. He once made a rash oath that almost cost the life of his son. Have you ever made a rash commitment or an offhanded promise—one you really had no intention of keeping? Whom do you think it harmed the most?

Saul was also deceitful. He offered his daughter's hand to David, hoping and fully expecting that David would die in battle. Saul also had a jealous streak. I guess he never understood that if you seek first the Kingdom of God, then all these things he was jealous for and of would be added unto his storehouse. Saul was also quite upset over being compared by the people to David, and he demonstrated his anger by pursuing and repeatedly attempting to kill David. Aaaahhhhhh! Finally, here it is, the intoxicating effects of power. I think one of the more well known comparisons was "Saul has killed his thousands and David his ten thousands." I guess Saul didn't realize that honor begets honor and that his reputation was not diminished by that comparison. A leader's duty in life is to pass on to the next generation better leaders than those that existed before his time and even better than he himself can claim to be.

Now let's take a look at the barriers David had to remove in order to succeed. First, there was his family. When Samuel asked Jesse to gather his sons so God could reveal the next king, nobody in the family thought to include the inconsequential David. Test yourself and see if you can answer the question how many of our country's greatest leaders came from underprivileged beginnings? God has a way of confounding the proud and intellectually superior while using the humble and insignificant—and, I might add, the reluctant—to do his best work. When David visited his brothers on the battle lines, he was scorned by them. Have you ever forgotten that dynamite comes in small packages or that diamonds are not all that big? When David took umbrage at Goliath's blasphemy, he was chastised by his brothers and told to go home. This advice, thankfully, was ignored. Sometimes doing the right thing will not really be the most popular thing. Even his leader Saul continually tried to sabotage David's effectiveness and eventually tried to kill him several times. Yet David's loyalty to his God and to the leadership of his commander did not waiver.

Yes, David faced many personal boundaries, but, with the aid of God, he always found ways around them. He did not come from the most royal of backgrounds, as he was from a poor family of shepherds and was the youngest of the sons. His age alone, though, was not truly a barrier, since he was not the only youngest son ever to be chosen by God to lead his people. David's youth and inexperience *were,* however, initially viewed by many as limitations, since he had never fought a battle. Yet he went from leading sheep to fighting Goliath after Samuel's anointing. Time and again he was disrespected and underestimated, much to the chagrin of those who did so.

So you see, it is not a question of having personal boundaries; every leader has them. It is, though, a matter of acting like David and raising those ceilings or those perceived barriers. What will you choose to do?

Chapter XXII

Josiah, a leader Who Understood Personal Victory

In our last discussion, the initiating text will come from **II Chronicles 34:3–35:19**, where we are going to learn our lesson from a man named Josiah, who is remembered by most people who know about him as a triumphant leader.

Josiah knew that, before leaders can ever achieve any degree of real success, they must first win their internal battles. Similarly, victorious leaders must guide their teams to victory by helping them to resolve any internal dissension or interpersonal conflicts or rivalries that may exist.

You will find that leaders who have learned and adhere to the lessons taught by victory itself seldom rely on using a Plan B, although they always have one standing by. These men are the types of leaders who find defeat so distasteful and unacceptable that they will continue striving for victory until they no longer possess a breath of life within them.

Winning battles, we have learned, takes a team, and a team requires a leader; therefore, it will always be the leader who must first ensure that all the team's members have conquered themselves before asking the team to undertake and conquer any cooperative task. How can a leader do this? Let's see, shall we, as we examine the impacts of "The Gift of Victory"?

Let's start with the thought that any leader who seeks to become a victorious leader must maintain an open and teachable mind. Leaders, who continue to learn are dynamic and will continue to grow with the times, constantly improve, achieve much, and habitually succeed. Josiah, unlike many current-day sixteen-year-olds, was willing to humble himself and sought God's ways over the arrogant ways of his father. Ouch, that hurt, because I had that same tendency early on as a parent—the inclination to be a bit arrogant when dealing with my family, especially my children. I think the seed of that arrogance was planted when I was a child, and my USMC father used to tell me, "Because I said so, and that is enough reason for anyone." I know for a fact the attitude was "watered" by both my Marine Corps career and my law enforcement career. As I matured in so very many ways—a process that is as yet incomplete—I have also found that there are leaders who for what ever reason, often treat their subordinates like they are children. I know that subordinates sometimes bring this on themselves, but that still doesn't make for a good working relationship.

Sometimes I wonder, though, just how many boys growing up today realize they are blindly emulating their fathers, no matter what kind of example they set and no matter what the cost? I can tell you, after responding to domestic disputes and domestic violence complaints for nearly forty years now, that the number is far too high. The legacy we are passing along to the next generation is more of a curse than a blessing. I think that, in many cases today, when a boy hears the phrase, "You're just like your father," it is not always meant as a compliment; more likely it carries the sting of a criticism issued by a distressed and frustrated mother.

In any case, embryonic leaders must realize, if they are to become great leaders, that, unless they are championing the right cause and expressing their passion for the right reasons and in the proper manner, they will rarely return from their battles bearing the triumphant mantle of the victor.

In addition, they must shed themselves of any and all the personal baggage they have carried with them from the past that will tarnish their image or damage their character. All leaders will, by their nature, hang on to some form of negative baggage; as you rise and seek to claim victory in your life and organization, you must get rid of these personal unrepented sins, damaging personal behaviors, past errors in judgment, and ungodly aspirations. Wherever you are in your leadership journey, you will eventually need to resolve these problems in your own life or you will never lead your team to a final victory. In fact, you will never really be a part of a team if you only consider yourself and your own desires; you can be a part of a gang or a mob, yes, but a team, no.

Real winning leaders must always recognize just what they need to give their followers and give it willingly. I have pointed out already that leaders must embrace personal sacrifice when necessary for the good of all and that victory does not come without someone paying a price. Think of why we are free today either as Christians or as Americans. Neither of these freedoms was achieved nor were they secured to our posterity, without someone being willing to pay the lofty price of spilled innocent and just blood, were they?

Leaders must always set the example of what they want their followers to become. At the heart of any organization is an example of what that organization's personality reflects. In other words, the leaders who are responsible for the organization's development are in fact the core of what establishes the character and subsequent worth of any organization. There is an old saying that has been proved valid more often than not, that states, "As the twig grows, so grows the tree."

Leaders must possess and express a strong personal commitment to success. Followers who are capable of forming their own commitments before their leaders are willing or able to make theirs will routinely look for other stronger leaders to follow or other organizations to join. Remember, commitment is contagious, and leaders need to control and direct the commitment of their followers, not follow the commitments of their subordinates. When followers are exposed to weak commitments and weak leadership, they lose their focus, their motivation, and their momentum. That sounds like a recipe for disaster, doesn't it? I know it isn't a formula for victory!

A leader always needs to help his or her followers succeed in their own personal battles and to homogenize them into a smoothly functioning team that is capable of enormous victories. There are many good ways to help them succeed in this endeavor. Here are just a few:

First, leaders need to know just where their followers are in regard to being ready for growth and changes to occur in their lives. Are the circumstances they are facing causing them to hurt enough to make them ready for a change? Have they learned enough from life to recognize how a change will benefit them, and do they want to attempt this change? Are they capable enough to effect a change? Answering these questions will help a leader develop his or her vision statement, which is the crux of a leader's mission planning.

Second, I also advocate praying for your people. I believe the old adage that goes, "There are no atheists in foxholes." I have shared many a foxhole and a few combat experiences with my brothers and sisters in the law enforcement and military communities, including service at home in America and in two overseas combat theaters of operation during my forty plus years in uniform. Although I realize that not everyone has come to call upon the Lord my God for his or her salvation, I have been reminded during many a chaotic incident of something the scriptures declare to be quite accurate. The saying "You receive not, because you ask not," is the one that comes to mind because I have heard many leaders softly praying under their breath, "God help me" or "Jesus save us," when things looked awfully bleak and it seemed that we were in hopeless circumstances. I might also remind you just how important a part the author Stormie Omartin thinks the **Power of Prayer** plays in our lives.

Third, leaders must also help their subordinates understand that both they themselves and the subordinates are human and, as such, are equally vulnerable to human frailties and equally need God's strength to make up any deficiencies that may exist in either of them. If they realize "from whence cometh your strength," they may very well seek to acquire God and his strength in their own lives.

Fourth, recognizing that humility fosters the efforts of a team, leaders of stature will ensure that their subordinates know they are not out to get all the glory. Good, strong leaders are not only willing to share the rewards of victory, but they continuously seek to find ways to recognize the efforts of all the members of their team. When the team members receive a message like this, then they, too, are more willing to share the spotlight with each other. A leader who advocates this approach begins building that proverbial band of brothers that is so frequently sought. This concept was one of Sun Tzu's basic principles and goes pretty far back in history as a keystone of effective leadership.

Fifth, Transparent leaders will always accept the responsibility for their shortcomings and for the shortcomings of their command. When leaders like these refuse to play the "blame game," their followers will do likewise, willingly sharing equally in the responsibility for the failure suffered or conquest achieved.

If a leader wants a winning team, that leader needs to have winning players—players as intent on achieving a victory as is their leadership. Are you the kind of leader who can stimulate the desire for victory in your subordinates? If not, when do you plan to start becoming one? Some of you folks must eventually step up and provide the continuity of leadership necessary to ensure the efficient and uninterrupted triumph of an entire organization, community, state, or nation and, without any disrespect intended, your family.

Chapter XXIII

"Hot Wash"
Leadership Performance Assessment

As we bring our leadership tutorial to a close, there are a couple things that I want you to pay special attention to as an up-and-coming leader. **First,** I want you always to bear in mind that, while you can, in fact, learn from your successes, more often than not they will be more effective in helping you teach others. It is my belief that you will learn much more from your mistakes, so never look at failure as anything but an opportunity to increase your potential. When you are successful in an endeavor, it is by and large because you already know what to do and how to do it. On the other hand, you will learn mountains from your mistakes, when you accept the responsibility for making them, that is. **Second,** never forget that that same maxim also holds true for those subordinates you lead. If you want to foster leadership in those around you, then develop a nurturing style of leadership, and do the world a favor: leave your road of life littered with germinating neophyte leaders, not their corpses.

The Marine Corps taught me a great deal about leadership, integrity, loyalty, and honor and gave me the opportunity, desire, ability, and moral courage to live my life with character, compassion, and conviction. As you continue to mature as a leader and continue experiencing life, you will acquire both a great deal of knowledge and an experiential understanding of life that, as you continue to develop, will mature into wisdom. That wisdom will, in due time, earn you the right to lead at whatever echelon you deserve.

No matter where you intend to exercise your newly tuned leadership skills—in your family, the business world, the military, or even in God's Army.

I leave you with my life's standard blessing:

"Firmus in Christo" and "Semper Fidelis"

"Steadfast in Christ" and "Always Faithful"

Until we meet again, I will continue serving

My God, My Family, My Country, and

My Corps.

Chief Warrant Officer 4

Gunner Ray R. Fairman, USMC (Ret.)

HONOR † FAITH † VALOR

Leadership Appendix

Mission-Ready Leadership Essentials from the "Ol' Gunner"

Just a few leadership reminders I picked up along my forty-two years, five months, and twelve days (but who's counting ...) of Marine Corps service. I hope they serve you as well as they have served to remind me just what my responsibilities really are.

If you want people to have confidence in you and your ability to lead, then you will have to show them you think they are more important than you are.

If you want to hold on to your subordinates' loyalty, then you better learn to let go of your own ego.

Truly great leadership ignores both personal gain and political expediency.

Great leaders rise to great heights, not on the backs of the subordinates whom they command, but by being carried on the shoulders of those subordinates they serve.

As a leader you should always remember as you climb the ladder of success that it was your fingers that once occupied the rung beneath your feet.

The leader who is faithful to the least of his duties will be trusted with even greater responsibilities, because it will be evident that he is more interested in leaving a legacy of other leaders in his wake, than in a monumental reputation.

I have trained many people in the Marine Corps and in law enforcement who have reached higher levels of leadership than I have. That, to me, is victory.

A leader must understand what it means to follow because it is a demonstrated fact that if you can't follow, you can't lead.

At all the military academies, leadership is always taught just like it is in boot camp, beginning with "Effective Followership 101."

*West Point and Annapolis have each produced more
real leaders than the Harvard Business School.*

Leadership is simply "influence," nothing more and nothing less.

*Discipleship, which is the art of training others to see, improve, and carry
on your vision ,is an art often sacrificed to the gods of personal insecurity.*

*Leadership suffers because we never allow our subordinates
to exercise their own potential because of our own
unhealthy fear of what might happen to us.*

*Subordinates have a right to expect their leaders to possess excellent
abilities and to be continuously increasing their competence.*

*Technical and tactical proficiency both belie mediocrity
and demand that a leader understand the meanings
of education, passion, and good, hard work.*

*Leaders who expect to earn the respect of their followers
must never do less than the absolute best job they can,
nothing more, and certainly nothing less.*

*Grounding your decisions on a firm foundation and not vacillating does
not mean never listening to others or being afraid to change your mind.*

*Great leaders surround themselves with other good
leaders and listen to their wise counsel.*

*Remember that you are not operating alone; even the leader is a part of
the team.*

*Never make your decisions based solely on emotion. If you do, they will
almost always come back to haunt you, as will decisions based on selfish
motives.*

*Leaders who let their situational ethics overpower their proper moral
decisions
will live to regret their compromises.*

Leadership is always power, but power is not always leadership.

The more of your leadership you invest in others, the stronger your leadership becomes.

Your influence increases not by hoarding power, but by wisely sharing it with those trusted subordinates you are training to someday take your place.

As you continue learning about life, you will gain both knowledge and experience,
which, as you mature, will turn to wisdom.

Wisdom will, in due time, earn for you the right to lead at whatever level you are worthy to do so.

Printed in the United States
215908BV00001B/5/P

9 781440 129810